Thinking Theory
BOOK THREE
Written by Nicola Cantan

www.colourfulkeys.ie

© 2016 Colourful Keys. All Rights Reserved.

WARNING! The contents of this publication are protected by copyright law.
To copy or reproduce them by any method is an infringement of the copyright law.

What is Thinking Theory?

→ Thinking Theory is a series of music theory workbooks designed to accelerate learning while providing plenty of reinforcement of each concept.

→ Thinking Theory is designed so you can start anywhere in the series. Concepts are not left out of later books, just covered more quickly.

Concepts covered in this book...

→ Note values: sixteenth note, eighth note, dotted eighth note, eighth note triplet, quarter note, dotted quarter note, half note, dotted half note & whole note

→ Rest values: sixteenth rest, eighth rest, quarter rest, half rest & whole rest

→ Time signatures: $\frac{2}{4}$ $\frac{3}{4}$ $\frac{4}{4}$ $\frac{2}{2}$ $\frac{3}{2}$ $\frac{4}{2}$ $\frac{3}{8}$ ₡

→ Landmark notes: low C, bass C, bass F, middle C, treble G, treble C & high C

→ Note stem rules

→ Grouping sixteenth notes, eighth notes & rests

→ Dynamics: pianissimo, piano, mezzo piano, mezzo forte, forte, fortissimo, crescendo, decrescendo, diminuendo, sempre forte, sempre piano & forte piano

→ Tempo marks: poco ritardando, poco rallentando, ritardando, rallentando, accelerando, a tempo, con moto, meno mosso, più mosso, presto, vivace, allegro, allegretto, moderato, alla marcia, andante, larghetto, largo, lento & adagio

→ Expression marks: giocoso, maestoso, espressivo, dolce, grazioso & cantabile

→ Markings/symbols: pedal, accidentals, staccato, slurs, repeat marks, fermata, accent, strong accent, tenuto, 1st and 2nd endings, 8va & 8vb

→ Solfa: low so, low la, low ti, do, re, mi, fa, so, la & high do

→ Scales: A minor, E minor, D minor, C major, G major, D major, F major & B♭ major

→ Triads: A minor, E minor, D minor, C major, G major, D major, F major & B♭ major

→ Intervals in the major scale

→ Whole steps, half steps & enharmonics

Contents

New concept pages are shown in bold.

Chapter 1	**Note/Rest Values & Time Signatures** 1	*Chapter 4*	**Grouping Notes & Rests** 22
	Dynamics 2		**Scales: A, E & D Harmonic Minors** 23
	Landmark Notes & Note Stems 3		Solfa Melody Completion 24
	Note Stem Drawing 4		Time Signatures 25
	Scales: C, G, D & F Majors 5		Grouping 26
	Solfa: Do, Re, Mi, Fa, So, La & Ti 6		Expression Marks 27
	Level Up! Chapter 1 Test 7		Level Up! Chapter 4 Test 28
Chapter 2	**Note Values** 8	*Chapter 5*	**Terms & Symbols** 29
	Grouping Notes & Rests 9		**Scales: A, E & D Melodic Minors** 30
	Solfa Singing 10		**Minor Triads** 31
	Major Triads 11		Triads 32
	Scales: B♭ Major 12		**Terms & Symbols** 33
	Tempo Marks 13		Solfa Melody Completion 34
	Level Up! Chapter 2 Test 14		Level Up! Chapter 5 Test 35
Chapter 3	**Time Signatures: ₵ 2/2 3/2 4/2 3/8** 15	*Chapter 6*	Level Up! The Final Test 36
	Intervals in Major Scales 16		Level Up! The Final Test 37
	Solfa: low so, low la & low ti 17		Level Up! The Final Test 38
	Scales: A, E & D Natural Minors 18		
	Grouping 19		
	Dynamics & Tempo Marks 20		
	Level Up! Chapter 3 Test 21		

About Nicola Cantan

Nicola Cantan began teaching piano in 2004, and has always strived to find new ways to engage students in learning. She uses games, improvisation and composing to accelerate her students' progress at the piano and broaden their musical knowledge.

Nicola wrote the 'Thinking Theory' books when she saw the struggle some of her students were having preparing for theory examinations. She wanted a book that regularly reinforced concepts in a systematic way, with a clean layout and clear explanations. Thus 'Thinking Theory' was born.

FLASHCARD GAMES

All the flashcard games can be played with the corresponding Thinking Theory Flashcards which can be downloaded at www.colourfulkeys.ie/thinking-theory.

To play these games, the cards will need to printed one-sided, with the answer on a separate card. You may want to print two sets, one to be used as regular flashcards (printed back to back) and one to be used for games (printed on one side).

You can play these games with the flashcards for one or more chapters at a time, or with the complete set for the whole book. Games like this are a fantastic way to reinforce learning off the page, and allow drilling of concepts in a fun way. Try to revisit each flashcard set periodically by playing a different game, to foster long term and reliable memory.

MEMORY

1. This is a game for one or more players.
2. Lay out all the cards face down.
3. Turn over two cards at a time. If they match, put those cards aside. If they don't match, turn them back over.
4. Keep going until all cards have been matched.

(This game can also be played with multiple players taking turns.)

MATCH

1. This is a game for one player.
2. Layout all the term cards face-up on the floor.
3. See how fast you can match the answer cards, by placing each card on top of the term that matches.
4. Time yourself and try to beat your time on the next go!

PAIRS

1. This is a game for two or more players.
2. Shuffle the cards and deal 4 to each player. Place the remainder of the cards in a pile between the players.
3. Each player takes turns to draw one card from the pile in the centre.
4. If s/he has a matching pair, s/he should place it face up beside them.
5. The winner is the one with the most pairs when all the cards have been drawn.

© Copyright 2016 Colourful Keys

SNAP

1. This is a game for two players.
2. Shuffle the cards and divide into two equal piles, one for each player.
3. On the count of three both players turn over the top card from her/his pile.
4. If the cards match, either player can shout "SNAP!".
5. The first player to say "SNAP!" wins all of the turned over cards, and adds them to her/his pile.
6. The winner is the first to win all the other cards, or the one with the most cards when time is up.

GO FISH!

1. This is a game for two or more players.
2. Shuffle the cards and deal 5 to each player. Place the remainder of the cards in a pile between the players..
3. Each player takes turns to ask another player for cards that would match one of her/his own. For example "Got any E's?" or "Got a crescendo?".
4. The player can continue asking for more cards until the other player does not have the card they need, and tells them to "Go fish!".
5. If told to "Go fish!" the player should pick up a card from the centre pile.
6. As pairs are found, they should be placed face down in front of them.
7. The winner is the first to get rid of all her/his cards. If two players do this at the same time, the winner is the one with the most pairs.

CUCKOO

1. This is a game for two or more players.
2. Remove one card from the deck and place it aside.
3. Shuffle the cards and deal all the cards between the players. It's OK if some players may get more cards than others.
4. Each player should sort through the cards and put down any pairs s/he finds, without letting the other players see her/his cards.
5. One player at a time offers her/his cards (face down) to the player to her/his left.
6. The player to the left takes one card from her/his hand.
7. If this makes a pair, the player to the left puts the pair down beside her/him.
8. Continue like this until all the pairs have been found. The player left with the "Cuckoo" is the loser.

New Ingredients: Rhythm

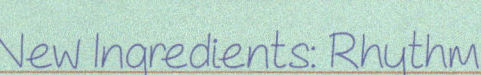
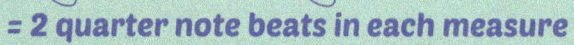

 Practice drawing the new ingredients.

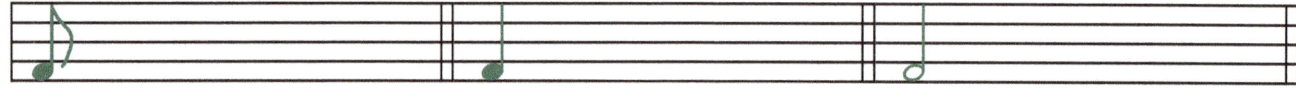
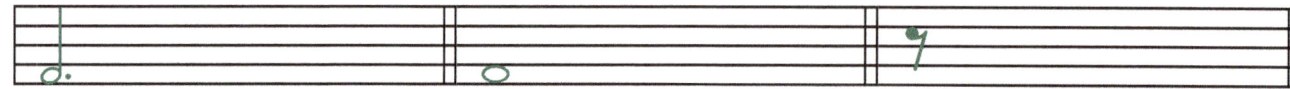
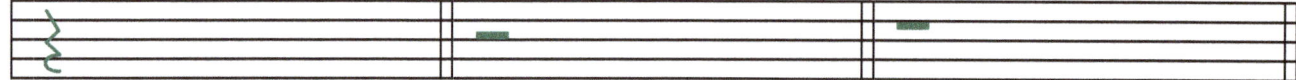
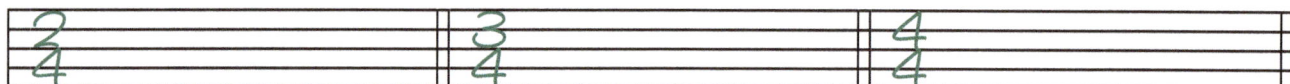

 Fill in the missing rests in these rhythms.

Practice clapping the rhythms.

< = crescendo = getting louder
> = diminuendo = getting softer
cresc. = crescendo = getting louder
dim. = diminuendo = getting softer
decresc. = decrescendo = getting softer

New Ingredients: Terms & Symbols

pp = pianissimo = very soft
p = piano = soft
mp = mezzo piano = moderately soft
mf = mezzo forte = moderately loud
f = forte = loud
ff = fortissimo = very loud

 Write the musical symbols in the boxes, from loudest to softest.

☐ → ☐ → ☐ → ☐ → ☐ → ☐

 Mark the statements as true or false.

Mezzo forte is softer than forte.	True ☐ False ☐
Decrescendo = diminuendo	True ☐ False ☐
Piano means play loudly.	True ☐ False ☐
Diminuendo = <	True ☐ False ☐
Pianissimo is louder than piano.	True ☐ False ☐
Fortissimo is louder than forte.	True ☐ False ☐
Mezzo forte means very loud.	True ☐ False ☐
Forte is softer than fortissimo.	True ☐ False ☐
Pianissimo means moderately soft.	True ☐ False ☐

 Translate these dynamics into Italian.

very soft = _____

getting softer = _____

very loud = _____

moderately loud = _____

getting louder = _____

Chapter 1   Thinking Theory Book Three

➜ Note Stem Rule 1: If the note is line 3 or above, the stem goes *down* on the *left* of the notehead. If the note is space 2 or below, the stem goes *up* on the *right* of the notehead.
➜ Note Stem Rule 2: The stem should finish at the same note an octave above for upward stems, and at the same note an octave below for downward stems.
➜ Note Stem Rule 3: Stems of notes more than one ledger line away from the staff finish at the middle line.

 Draw the notes below, taking care with stem lengths.

10 middle C quarter notes.

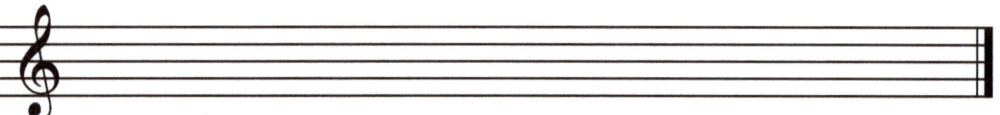

8 treble C whole notes.

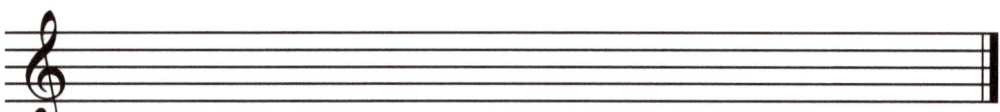

12 bass F half notes.

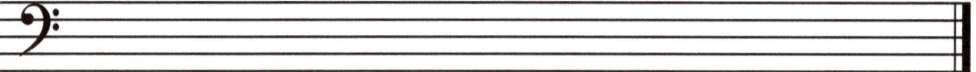

10 high C half notes.

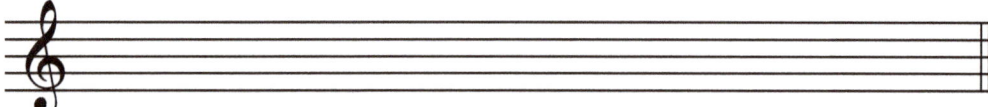

8 low C eighth notes.

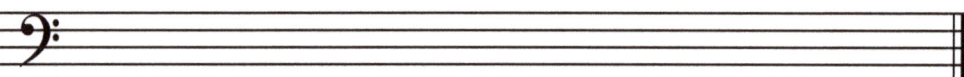

6 bass C dotted half notes.

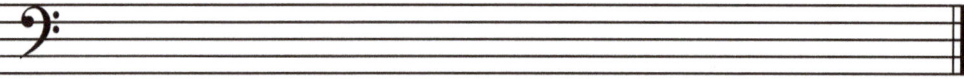

Chapter 1

→ We can use the landmark notes learned on the previous page to work out any other note. Simply work your way up or down the staff from the closest landmark note.

Identify each note below & add stems to make the noteheads into quarter notes.

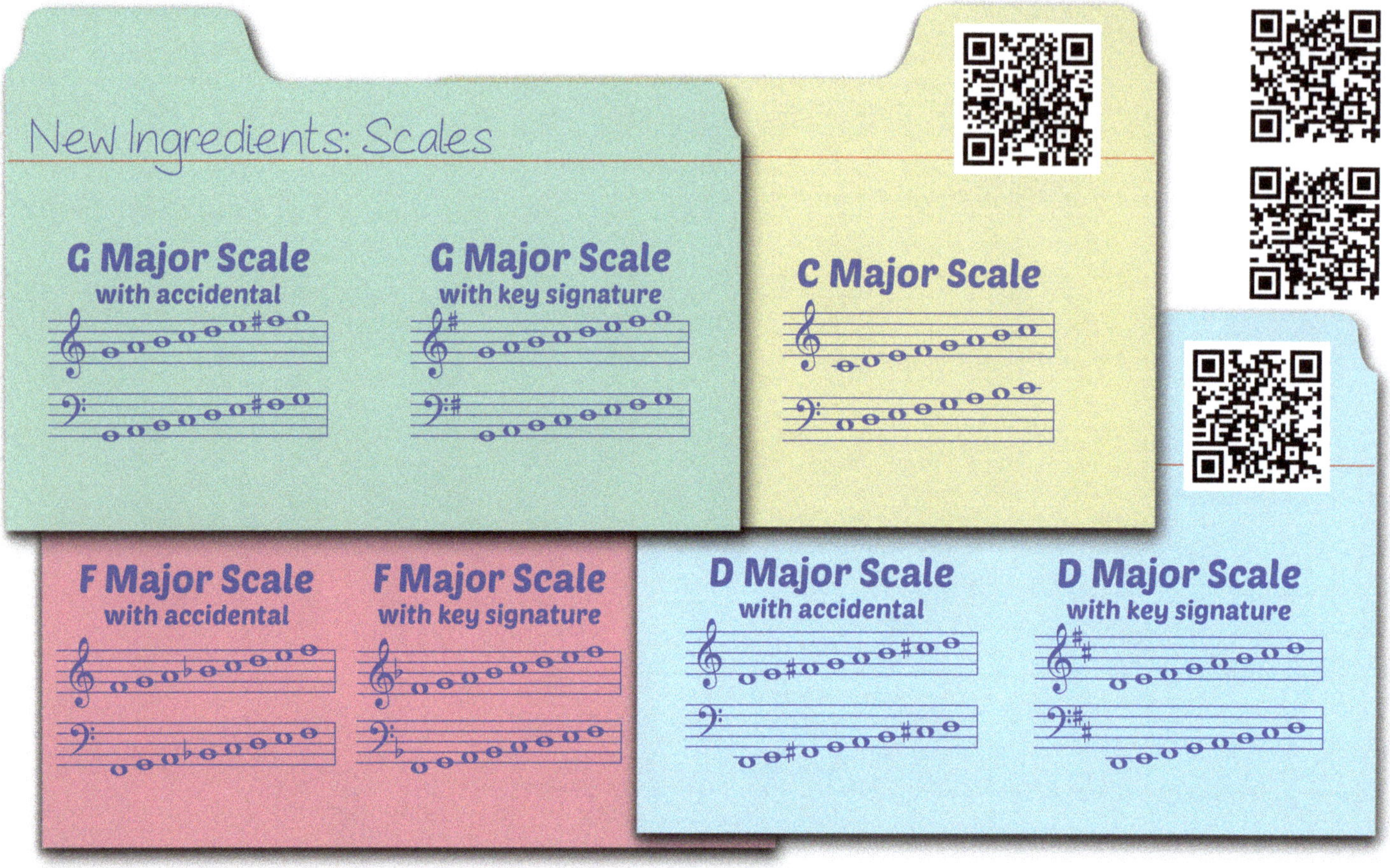

Chapter 1 — New Ingredients: Scales

G Major Scale with accidental
G Major Scale with key signature
C Major Scale
F Major Scale with accidental
F Major Scale with key signature
D Major Scale with accidental
D Major Scale with key signature

✏️ Write each scale, going down, in the treble & bass clef. Use key signatures. Color in the keys used in the scale on the keyboard.

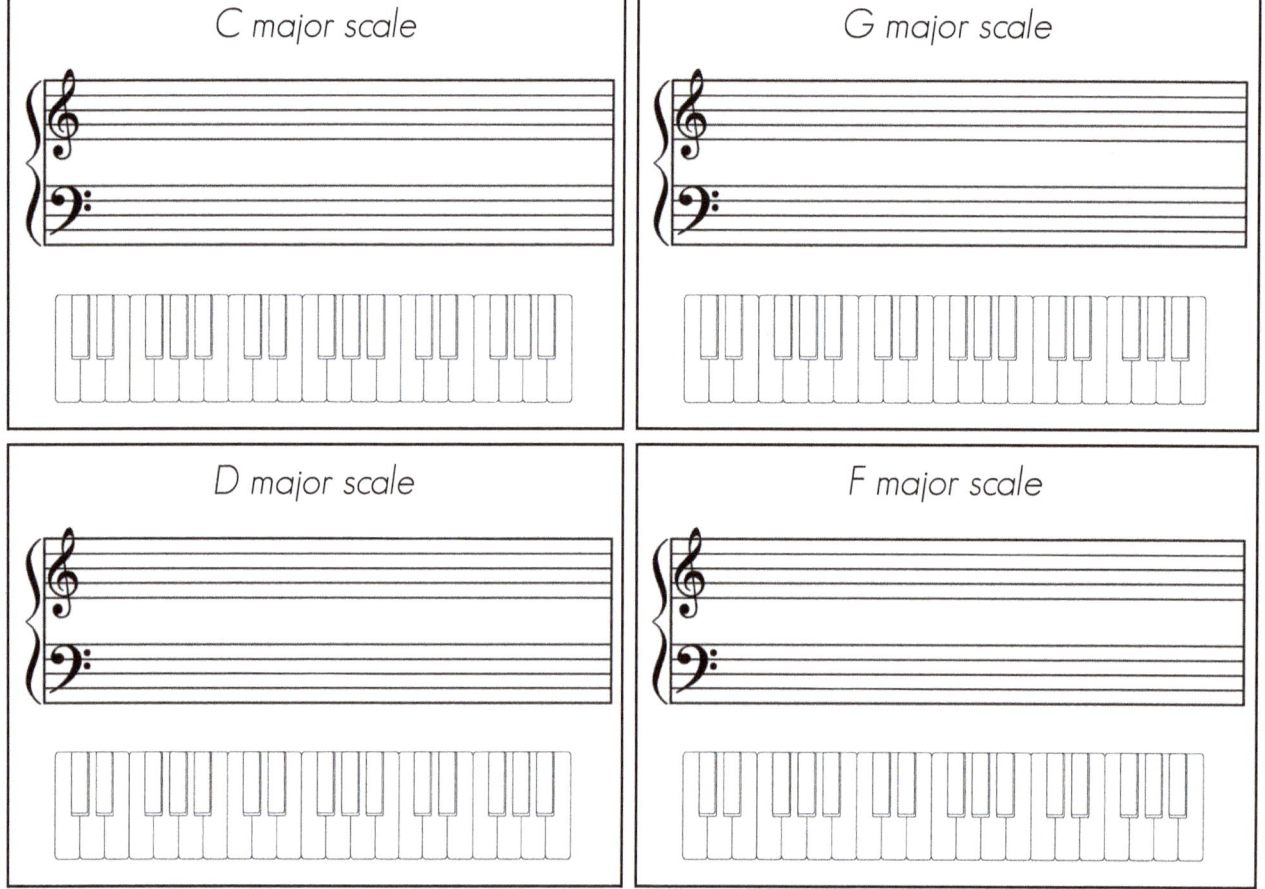

C major scale

G major scale

D major scale

F major scale

New Ingredients: Solfa

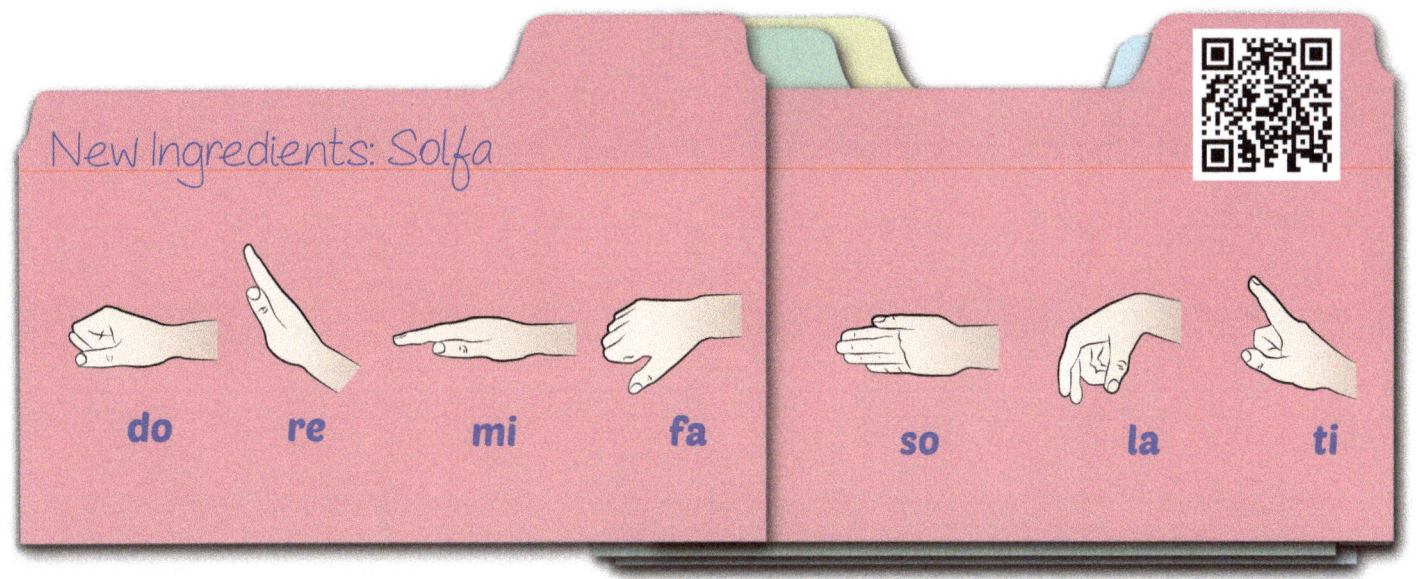

🗣 Practice singing the exercises below using the solfa hand signs.

Chapter 1   Thinking Theory Book Three

Level Up!
Get ready for chapter 2 by answering these questions (without looking back through your book!)

1. Add note stems to these quarter note heads, then write in the note names underneath.

2. Draw notes on the staff for each of these notes.

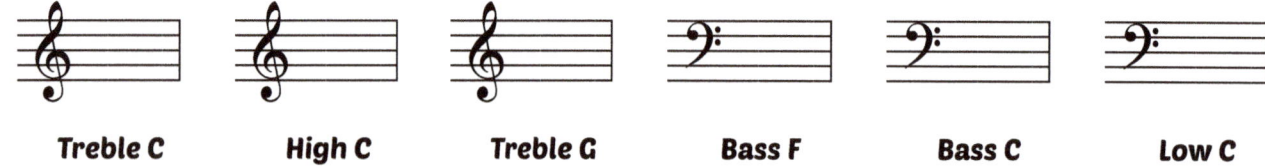

   Treble C   **High C**   **Treble G**   **Bass F**   **Bass C**   **Low C**

3. Write the time name and number of beats for each of these notes and rests.

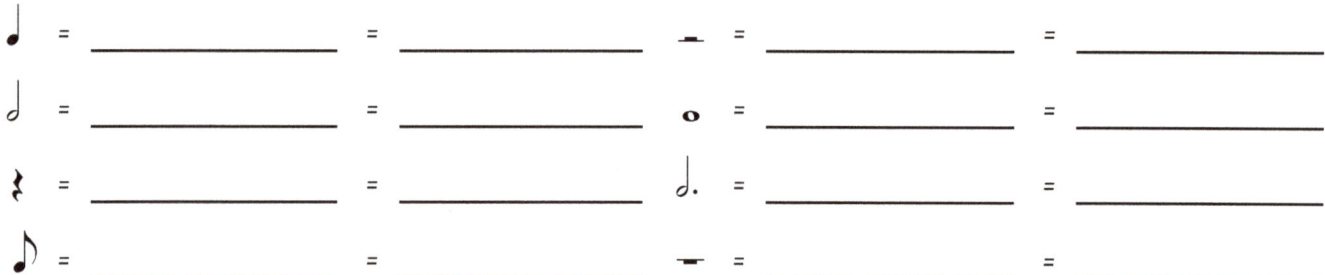

4. Label each solfa hand sign.

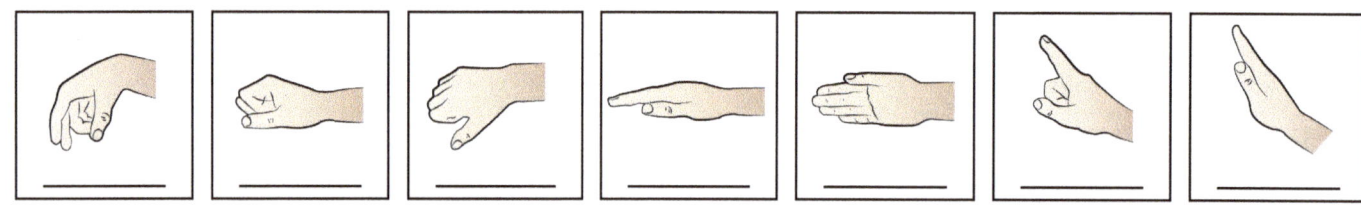

5. Write the scales to match these key signatures, in half notes, ascending and descending.

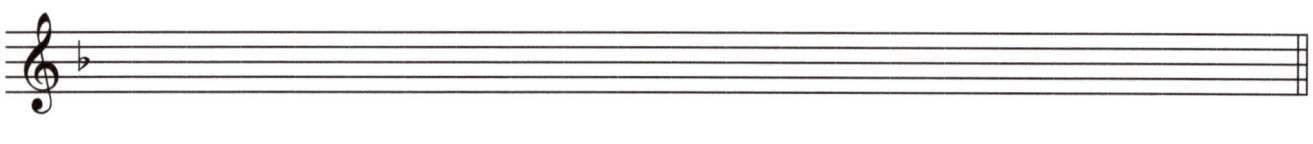

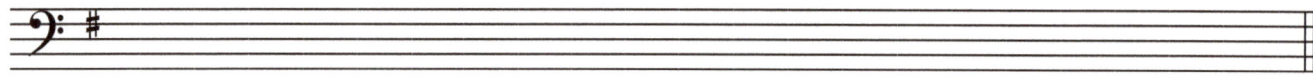

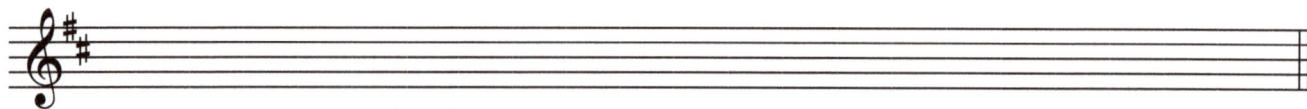

- A triplet divides a beat into three equal parts.
- The eighth note triplet divides a quarter note into three equal thirds.
- Eighth notes and sixteenth notes can be written separately with tails, or *beamed* together in groups.

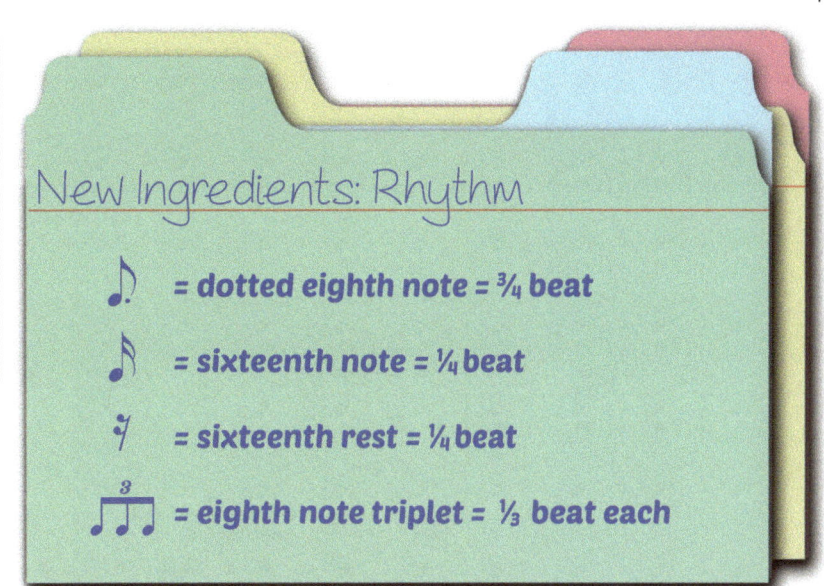

Try clapping the rhythm below, first saying the rhythmic syllables, then counting, then saying the words. Which do you find easiest?

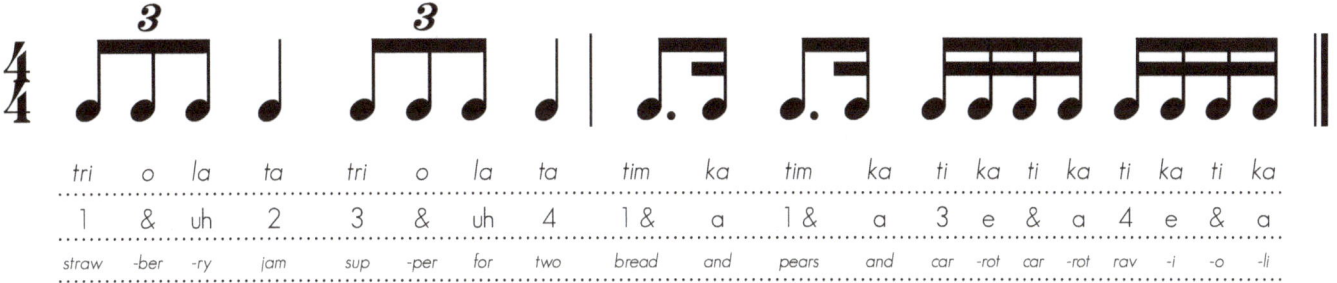

Fill in the counts under the rhythmic syllables. Write words for the rhythm. Practice clapping the rhythms using all three methods.

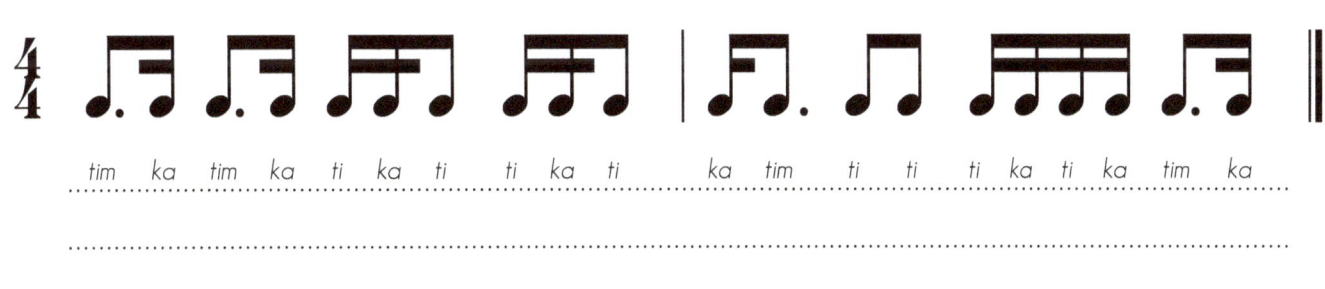

➜ Eighth notes and sixteenth notes are beamed or joined together in groups to make reading easier.
➜ In $\frac{2}{4}$, $\frac{3}{4}$ & $\frac{4}{4}$ eighth notes and sixteenth notes are grouped into quarter note beats.
➜ A whole measure of eighth notes can be beamed in $\frac{2}{4}$ & $\frac{3}{4}$.
➜ A half measure of eighth notes can be beamed in $\frac{4}{4}$.

Group/beam these eighth notes and sixteenth notes.

➜ Rests are grouped in a similar way to sixteenth note note and eighth notes.
➜ A rest for a whole measure is shown with a whole rest, no matter what the time signature is.

➜ In $\frac{2}{4}$ & $\frac{3}{4}$ each beat needs a separate rest.
➜ In $\frac{4}{4}$ a half rest is used for a silent half measure.

Fill in the missing rest/rests at the arrows below.

Practice clapping the rhythms.

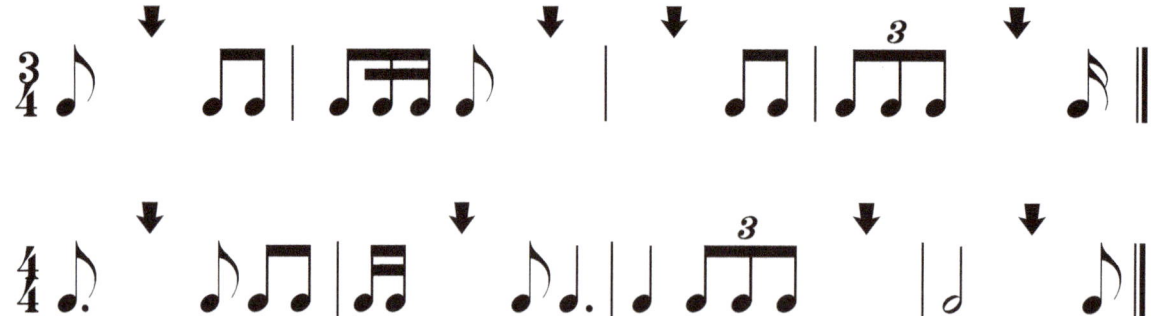

Thinking Theory Book Three — Chapter 2

> → To sing a complete major scale in solfa we need to add another 'do' an octave above the tonic. We write this high *do* as *d'*.

✏️ Label each note with its solfa initial.

✋ Practice singing the exercises below, using the solfa hand signs.

d

d

d

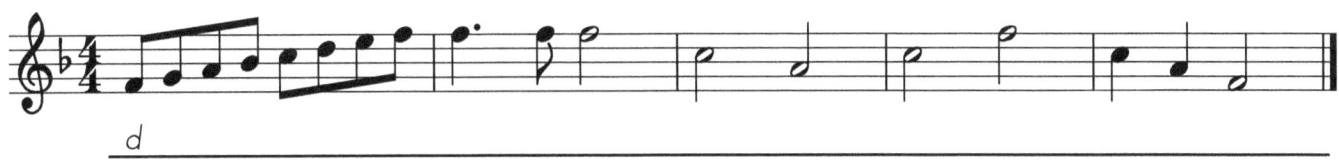
d

d

Chapter 2

> → The first note of any scale can be called the *keynote* or the *tonic*.
> → A *tonic triad* is made up of three notes: the first, third and fifth note of the scale played in unison.
> → In a major key these are the notes *do, mi* and *so*. You may know this combination of notes from playing arpeggios.

✏️ Draw the triads below in the treble and bass clefs. Use key signatures.

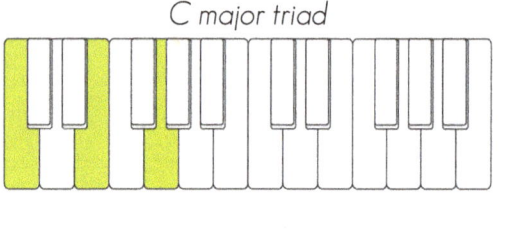

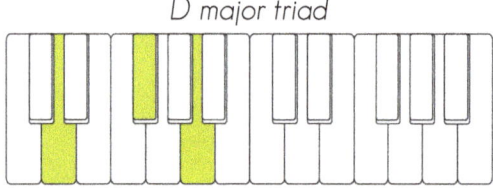

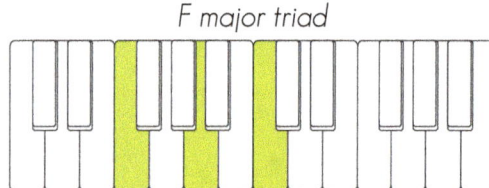

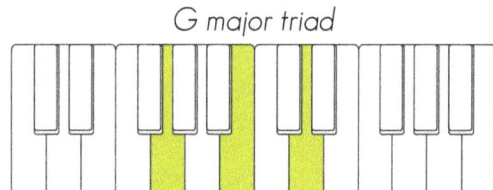

✏️ Write the full Italian term beside each of the symbols/letters below.

pp = _____   *mp* = _____

< = _____   *f* = _____

mf = _____   > = _____

ff = _____   decresc. = _____

Thinking Theory Book Three   Chapter 2

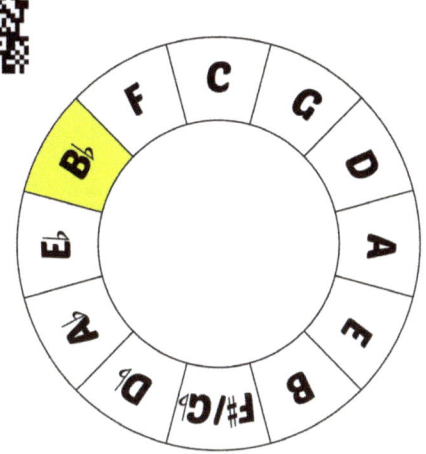
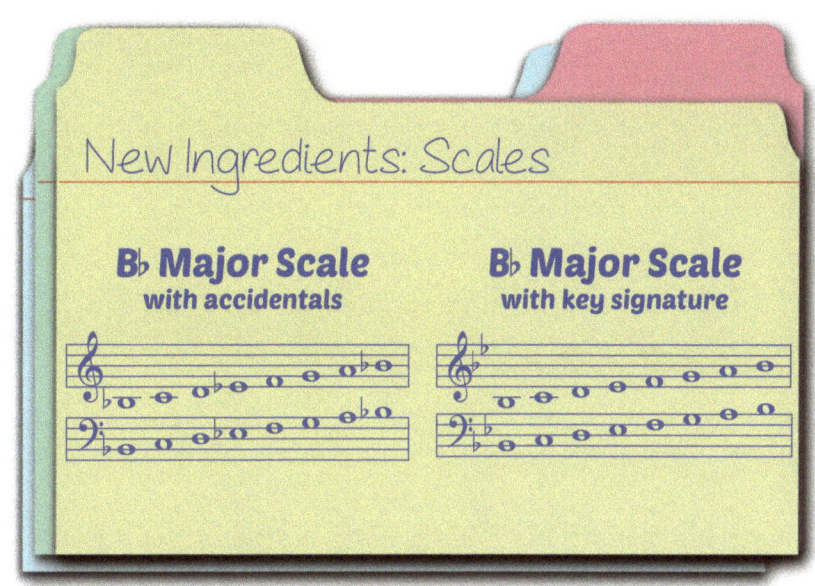

✏️ Color in the keys used in the B♭ major scale. Mark the whole and half steps.

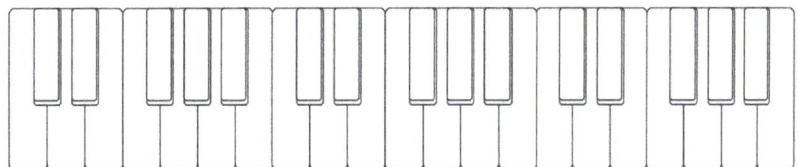

✏️ Finish this sentence.

    The B♭ major triad is made up of the notes __ , __ & __.

✏️ Rewrite these solfa notations on the staff, in the key of B♭ major.

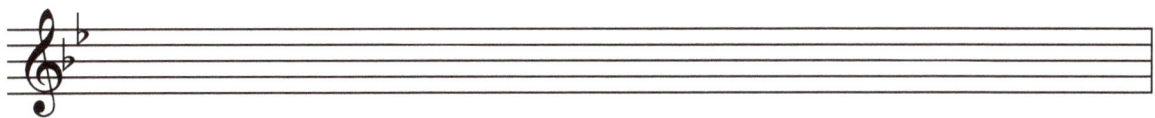

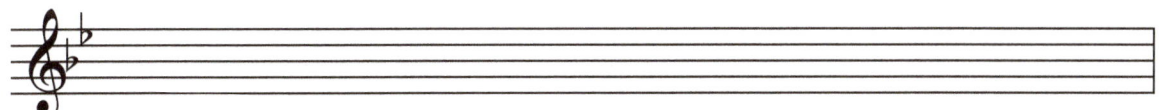

New ingredients: Terms & Symbols

allegro = quick & lively
allegretto = moderately quick & lively
moderato = moderate speed
andante = walking pace
largo = slowly
adagio = slowly

rit. = gradually getting slower
ritard. = gradually getting slower
rall. = gradually getting slower
poco rall. = gradually getting a little slower
poco rit. = gradually getting a little slower
accelerando = gradually getting faster
a tempo = back to original speed

✏️ Add markings to the score below to show that:

1. The piece should get faster from measure 4, and go back to the original tempo at measure 8.
2. The piece should be played at a moderate tempo.
3. The piece should begin very loudly.
4. The player should slow down a little for the last two measures.
5. The music should start to get gradually quieter at measure 6.

✏️ Give the time names for each of the note/rest values below.

𝐨 = _____   𝄾 = _____

𝄽 = _____   ♪. = _____

♪ = _____   ▬ = _____

3
♫ = _____   𝅗𝅥 = _____

Level Up!

Get ready for chapter 3 by answering these questions (without looking back through your book!)

1. Create major triads from each of the tonics below.

2. Draw the descending major scales to match each of these key signatures, in sixteenth notes.

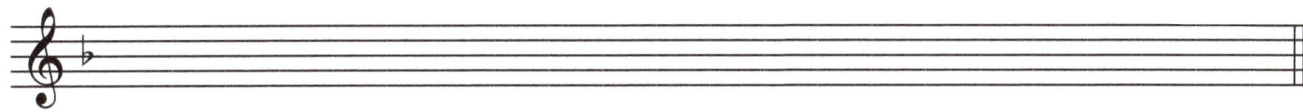

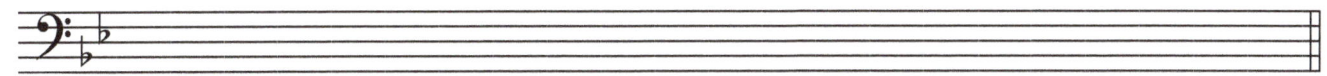

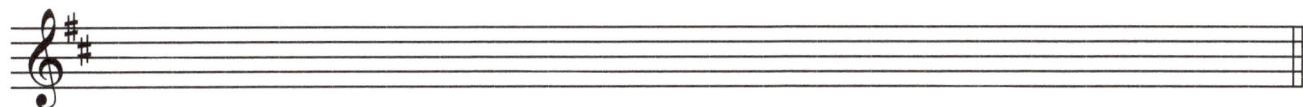

3. Rewrite this melody on the staff below, with the notes correctly grouped.

4. Fill in the meanings for each term below.

allegro = _____ *andante* = _____

accelerando = _____ *poco rall.* = _____

rall. = _____ *allegretto* = _____

largo = _____ *moderato* = _____

rit. = _____ *a tempo* = _____

adagio = _____ *poco rit.* = _____

Chapter 3

- Time signatures can use half or eighth note beats instead of quarter notes.
- Writing with a different type of beats does not change the sound, just the appearance.
- The sound of 2/4 & 2/2 for example is the same, but looks different.

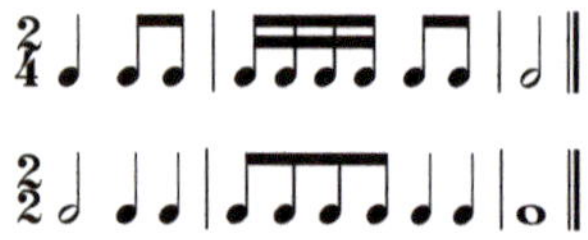

✏️ Draw the missing barlines in each tune.

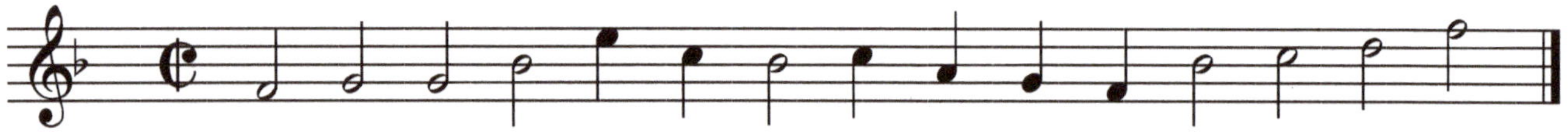

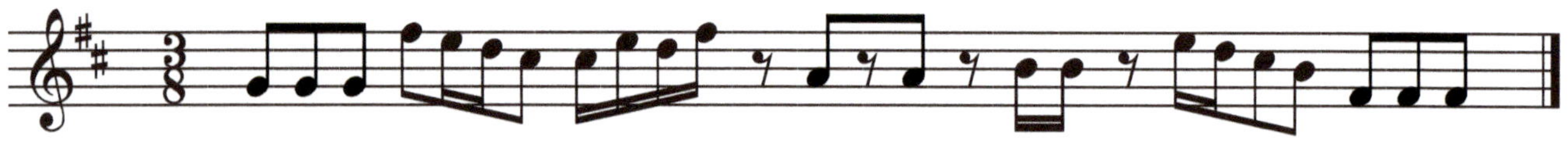

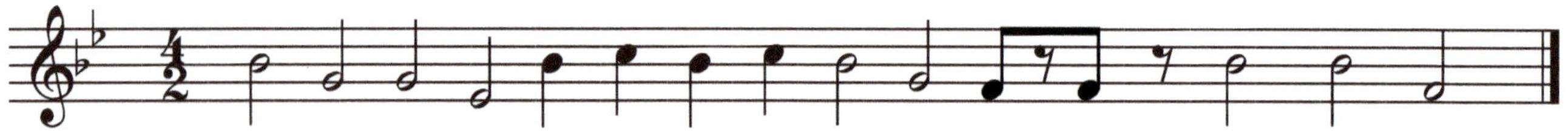

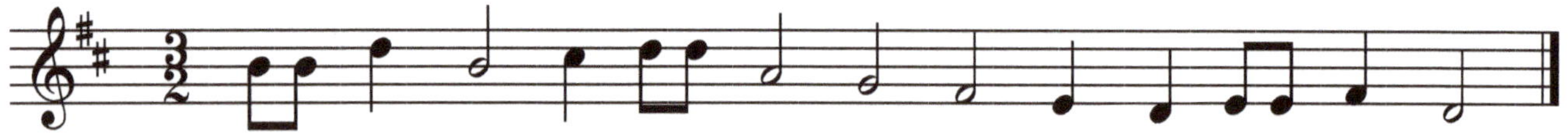

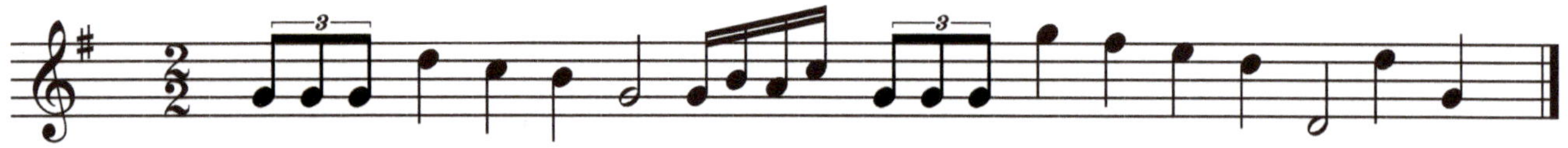

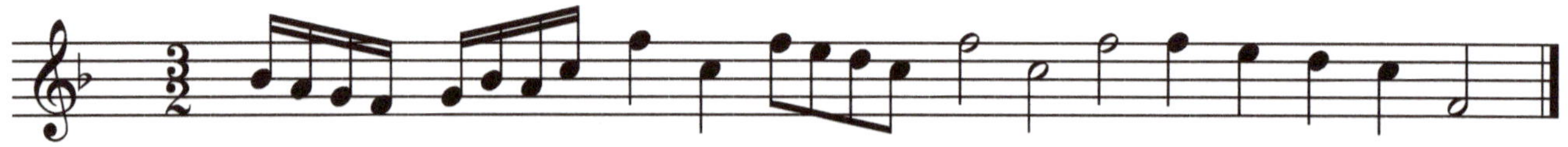

- An interval is the distance between two notes.
- For now we will only be dealing with intervals from the tonic of a scale.
- A *harmonic interval* is the distance between two notes which sound together.
- A *melodic interval* is the distance between two notes which sound one after the other.

✏️ Draw notes above the given notes to create harmonic intervals from the major scale. Label each one as major or perfect.

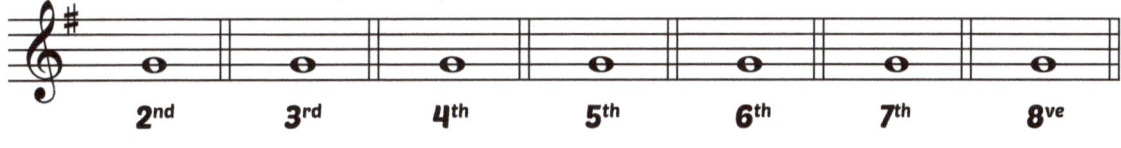

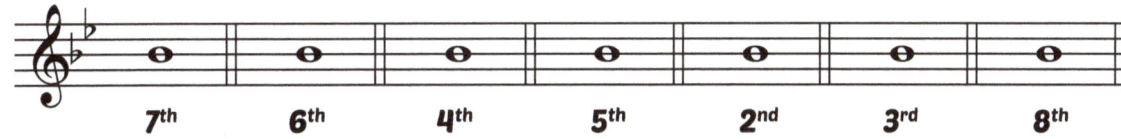

✏️ Draw notes beside the given notes to create melodic intervals.

Chapter 3 — Thinking Theory Book Three

> → To show a solfa note lower than the tonic, we use a small tick after the solfa initial to indicate a low note.
> → The three most commonly used low notes are s, l, t,

🗣 Practice singing the exercises below to get used to these new notes.

d s, d s, d d s,   d s, s, d s, s, s, d

d l, d l, d l, d   d t, d t, d t, t, d

d s, s, d d s, d   s, s, s, s, d

d d l, d l, l, d   d t, d t, t, d t,

d s, d s, s, d d s,   d s, s, s, s, d d

d l, l, d d l, d   d t, t, d t, t, t, d

✏️ Fill in the solfa initials under the notes.
🗣 Practice singing the exercises.

d

d

d

d

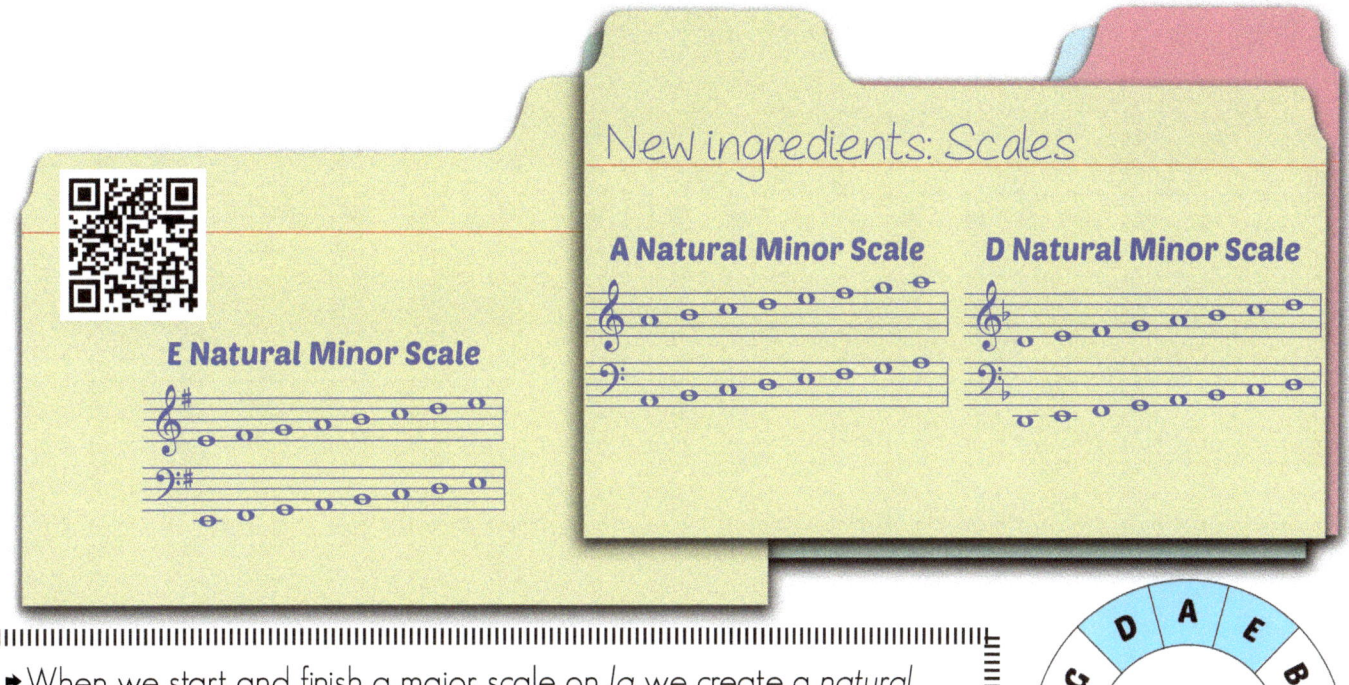

- When we start and finish a major scale on *la* we create a *natural minor* scale.
- Major and minor scales built from the same key signature are described as *relatives*.

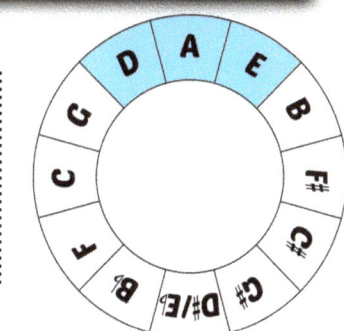

✏️ Write each scale, in half notes, going down, using accidentals, in the treble & bass clef. Color in the keys used in the scale on the keyboard.

E natural minor scale

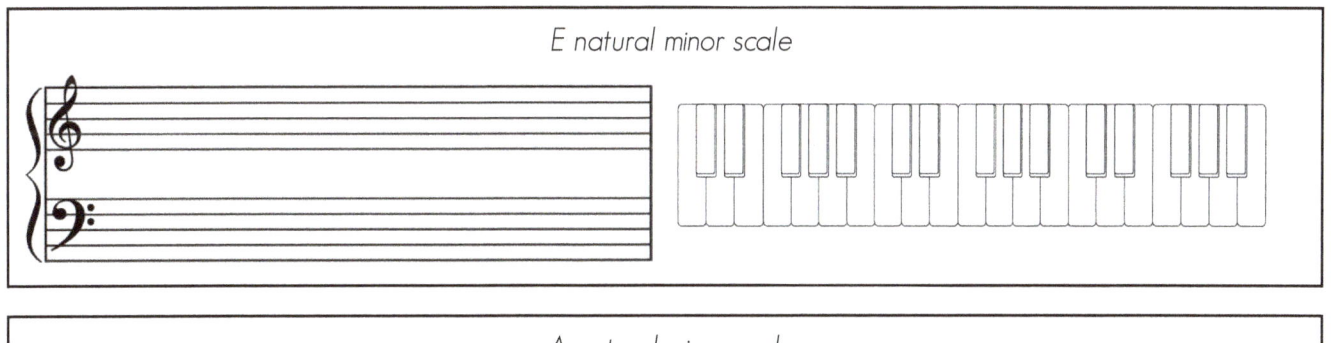

A natural minor scale

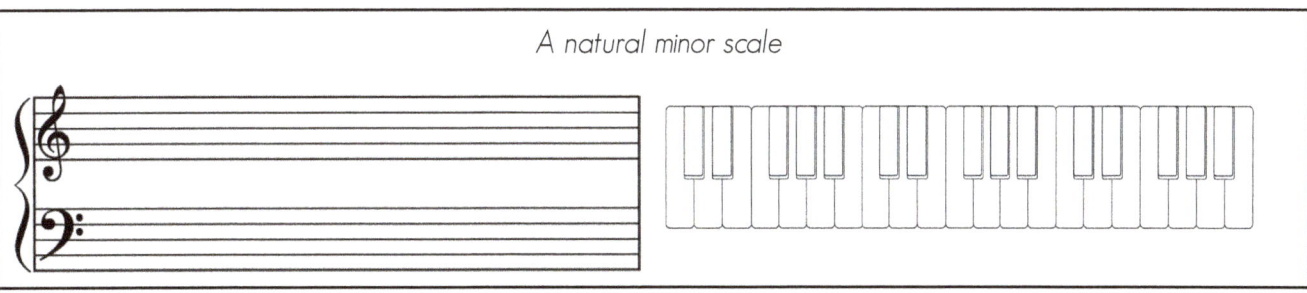

D natural minor scale

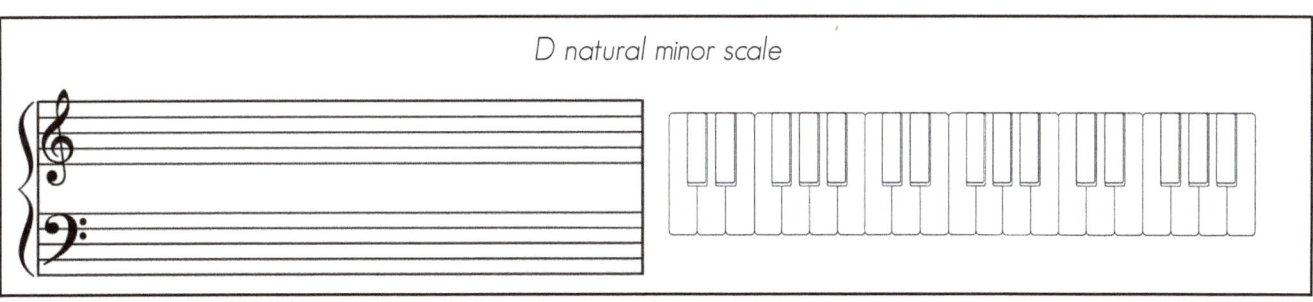

✏️ Redraw the solfa notation on the staff, in the key of D major.
Add the clef, time signature and key signature. Take care with grouping.

✏️ Redraw the solfa notation on the staff, in the key of F major.
Add the clef, time signature and key signature. Take care with grouping.

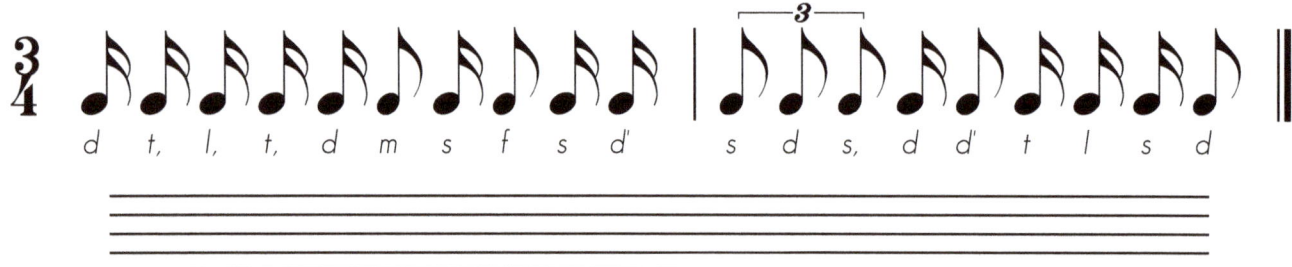

✏️ Redraw the solfa notation on the staff, in the key of B♭ major.
Add the clef, time signature and key signature. Take care with grouping.

✏️ Redraw the solfa notation on the staff, in the key of G major.
Add the clef, time signature and key signature. Take care with grouping.

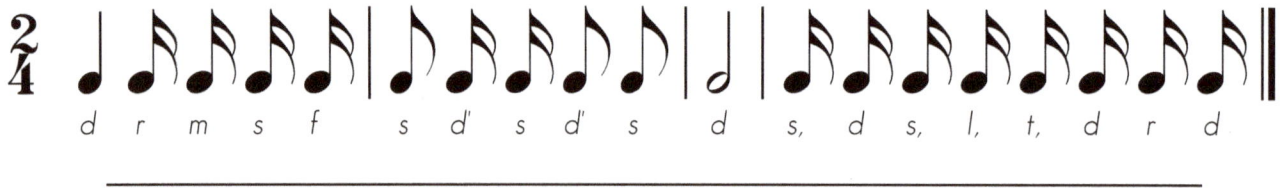

New ingredients: Terms & Symbols

Lento = slow
Larghetto = fairly slow
Alla marcia = like a march
Vivace = lively
Presto = fast

sempre f = sempre forte = always loud
sempre p = sempre piano = always soft
sf = emphasized
fp = loud then immediately soft
con moto = with movement
meno mosso = less movement/slower
più mosso = more movement/faster

 Answer the questions below.

1. What does *moto* mean? _____
2. What does *sempre* mean? _____
3. Is *vivace* slower or faster than *largo*? _____
4. What does *più* mean? _____
5. Is *presto* slower or faster than *vivace*? _____
6. What does *meno* mean? _____
7. Is *larghetto* slower or faster than *alla marcia*? _____

 Fill in the Italian terms that match each of the definitions below.

like a march = _____   getting softer = _____

getting louder = _____   with movement = _____

original speed = _____   very soft = _____

quick & lively = _____   slow = _____

more movement = _____   moderately soft = _____

getting slower = _____   walking pace = _____

moderate speed = _____   fast = _____

Level Up!

Get ready for chapter 4 by answering these questions (without looking back through your book!)

1. Identify each of these intervals.

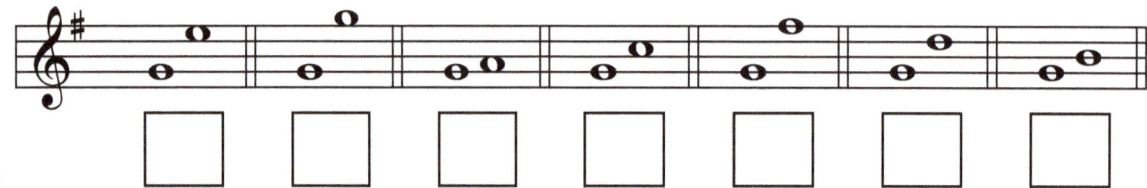

2. Are these notes whole steps, half steps or enharmonics? Circle 'W', 'H' or 'E'.

3. Write the scale of E natural minor, ascending, in the bass clef. Use a key signature.

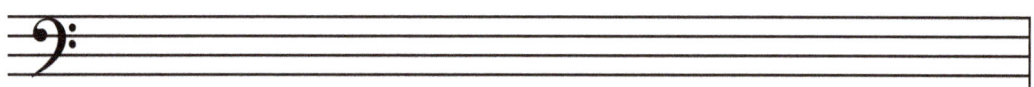

4. Draw the missing note values to complete the measures.

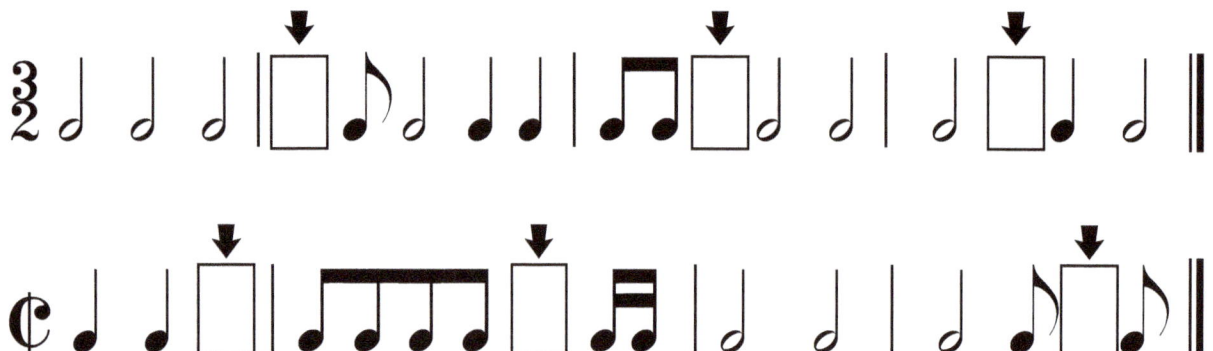

5. Fill in the meanings for each of these symbols.

alla marcia = _____   fp = _____

sf = _____   larghetto = _____

sempre p = _____   vivace = _____

dolce = _____   diminuendo = _____

Draw a note above each given note to create harmonic intervals.

 Draw a note beside each given note to create melodic intervals.

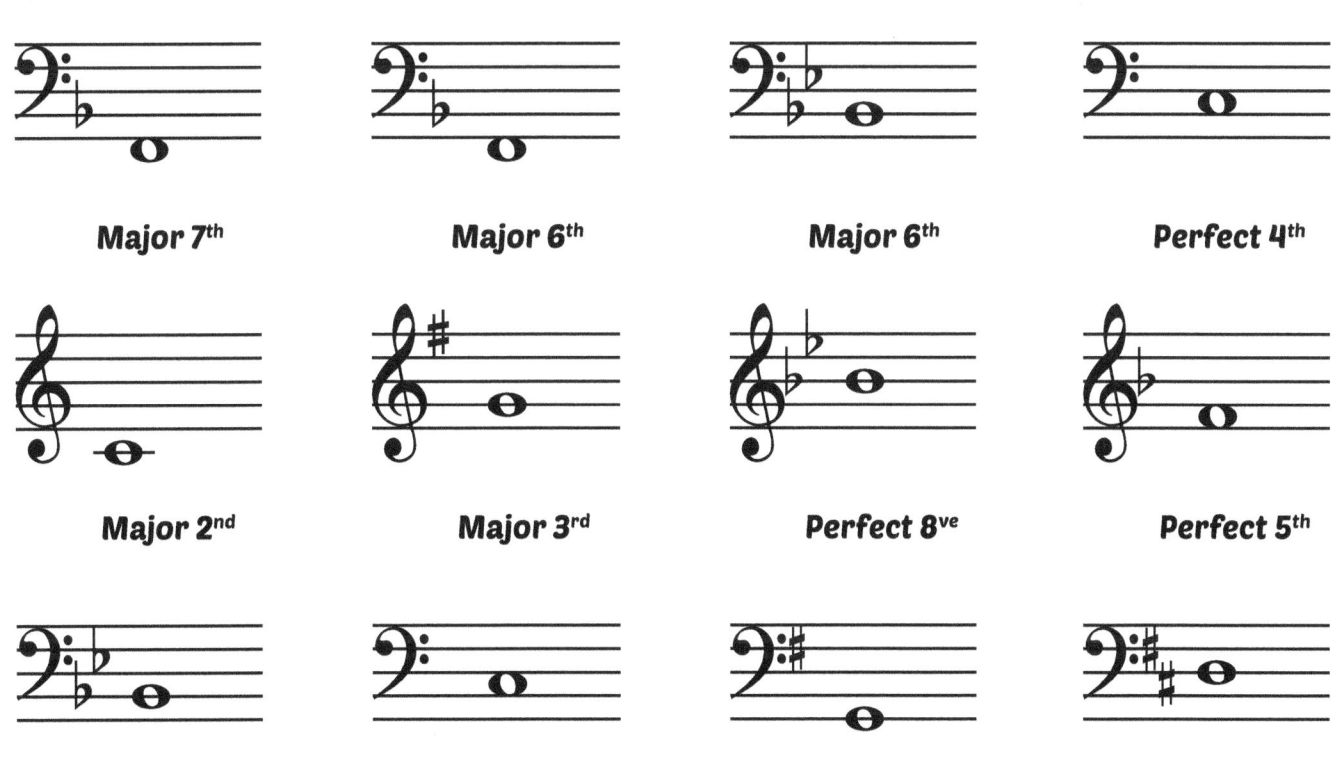

Chapter 4

> ➜ To make a *harmonic* minor scale from a *natural* minor scale, raise the seventh scale degree (so) one half step.
> ➜ In solfa we call this note 'si'.

✏️ Write each scale, in quarter notes, going down, in the treble & bass clef. Color in the keys used in the scale on the keyboard.

A harmonic minor scale

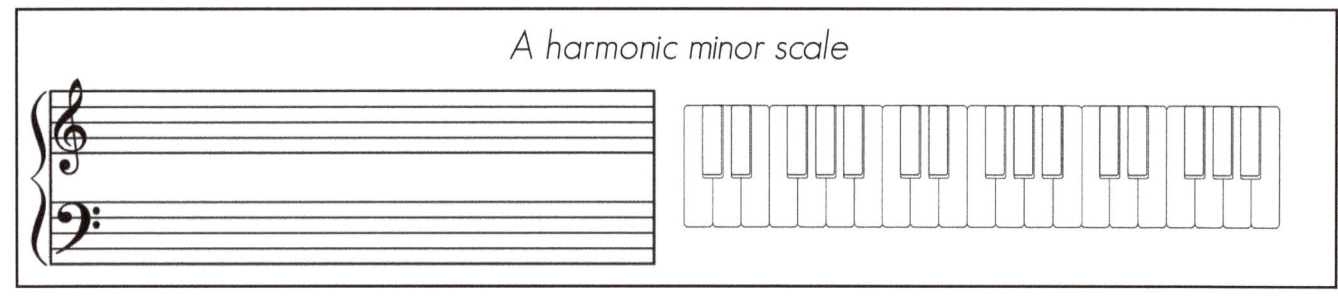

D harmonic minor scale

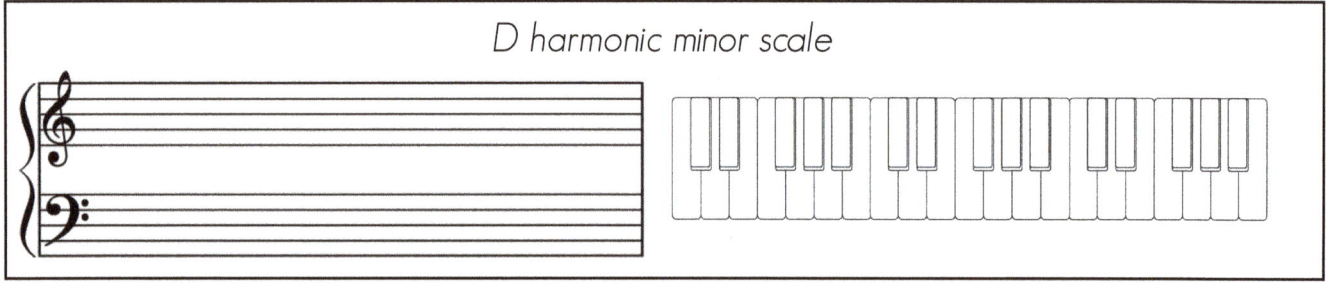

E harmonic minor scale

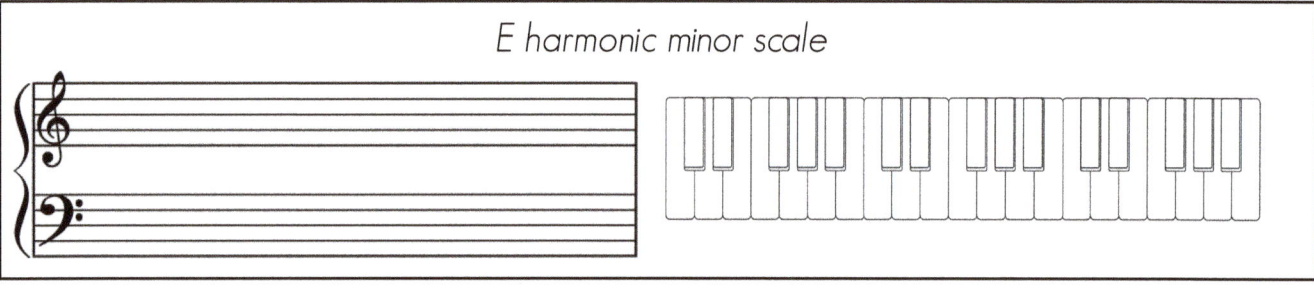

✏️ Label the notes of these harmonic minor scales with solfa.

👄 Practice singing the exercises.

la

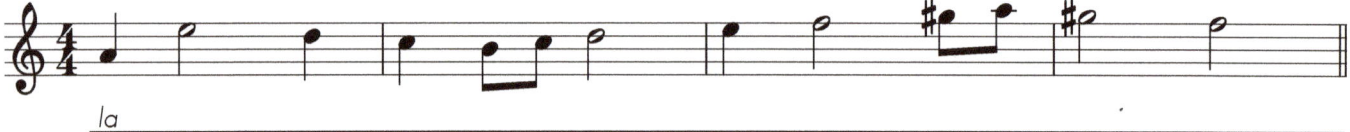
la

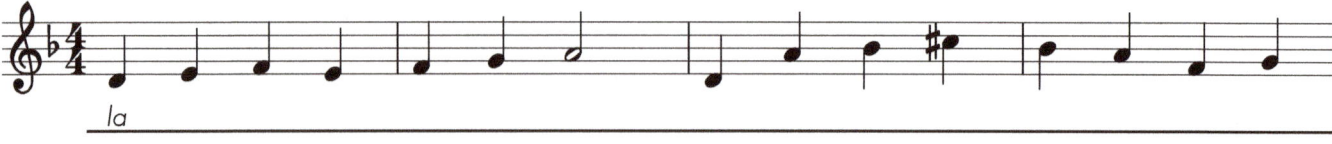
la

Chapter 4

- Singing a melody using solfa will help you to compose an ending for it.
- Most melodies will sound best if they end on a long *do*.
- Draft your ideas in solfa stick notation before writing them on the staff.

✏️ Finish each melody by composing another two measures. Add a *tempo* mark above the staff, and a *dynamic* mark below the staff, to suit each melody.

✏️ Label each of these time signatures as simple or compound and duple, triple or quadruple.

¢	4/2	C
___ ___	___ ___	___ ___

2/2	3/4	2/4
___ ___	___ ___	___ ___

3/2	4/4	3/8
___ ___	___ ___	___ ___

✏️ Compose 4 measures of rhythm for each of the time signatures below.
👏 Practice clapping the rhythms.

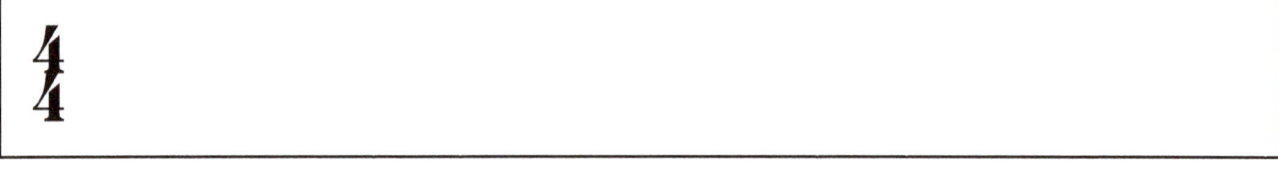

3/2

Label each of these triads.

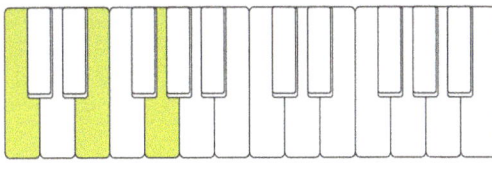   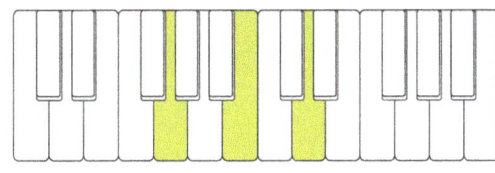

_____   _____

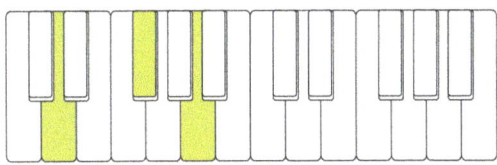   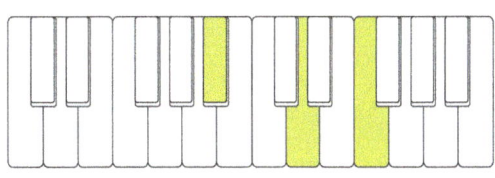

_____   _____

 Make these tonics into major triads by adding two more notes.

Chapter 4 — New Ingredients: Terms & Symbols

dolce = sweetly
grazioso = gracefully
cantabile = with a singing tone
giocoso = playful/merry
maestoso = majestic
espressivo = expressive

✏️ Write one Italian term under each image that best represents it.

_____   _____   _____

_____   _____   _____

✏️ Translate each of these terms.

Vivace = _____   **adagio** = _____

sempre f = _____   **Larghetto** = _____

più mosso = _____   **a tempo** = _____

Lento = _____   **Presto** = _____

Level Up!

Get ready for chapter 5 by answering these questions (without looking back through your book!)

1. Add the missing time signature to each melody. Describe each time as duple, triple or quadruple.

_____

_____

2. Write the key signature and one octave of each scale. Mark the half steps.

E harmonic minor ascending

D major descending

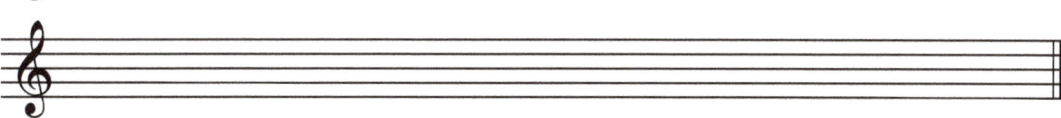

B♭ major descending

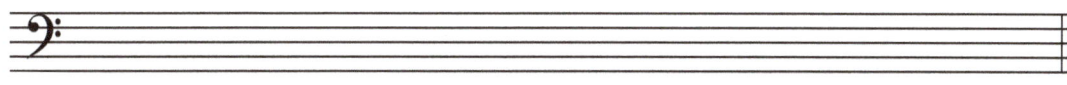

D natural minor descending

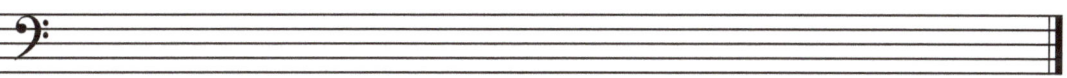

3. Translate each of these musical terms into Italian.

sweetly = _____   lively = _____

playful = _____   gracefully = _____

singing tone = _____   majestic = _____

expressive = _____   fast = _____

4. Give the time name for each of these notes.

♪. = _____   ♩ = _____

♬ = _____   (triplet eighths) = _____

♩ = _____   𝅝 = _____

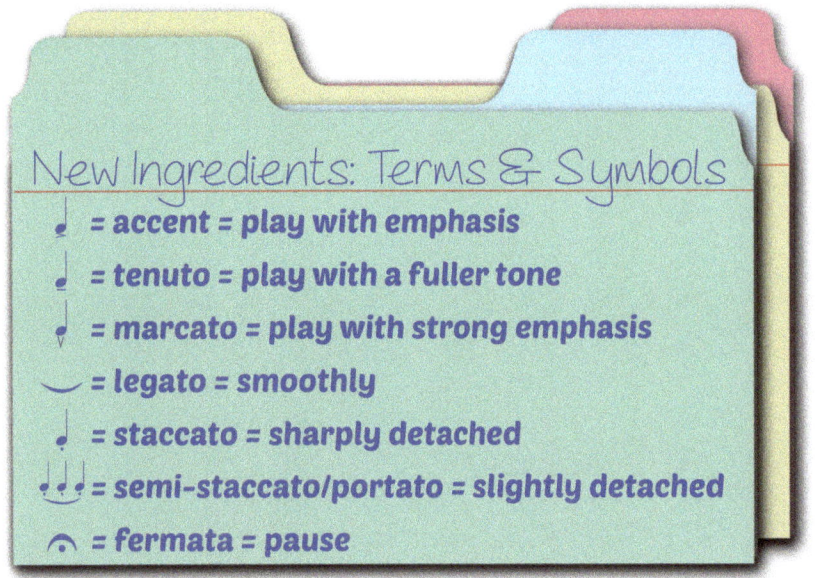

 Add the missing time signature to the musical example below.

 Add markings to the score below to show that:

1. The dotted quarter note in measure 2 should be stressed.
2. The treble clef notes in measures 1 & 7 should be played portato.
3. The piece should be played playfully.
4. The player should pause on the final note of measures 4 & 8.
5. The piece should start very loudly, get softer from measure 4, and finish loudly in measure 8.

 Answer these questions about the piece.

1. What major key is the piece in? _____
2. Is the time signature duple, triple or quadruple? _____
3. Is the time signature simple or compound? _____

Chapter 5

- To make an ascending *melodic* minor scale from a *natural* minor scale, raise the sixth & seventh scale degrees (*fa* & *so*) one half step.
- In solfa, we call these new notes '*fi*' and '*si*'.
- The *natural* minor is used when descending in *melodic* minor.

✏️ Write each scale, in half notes, ascending & descending, in the clef given.

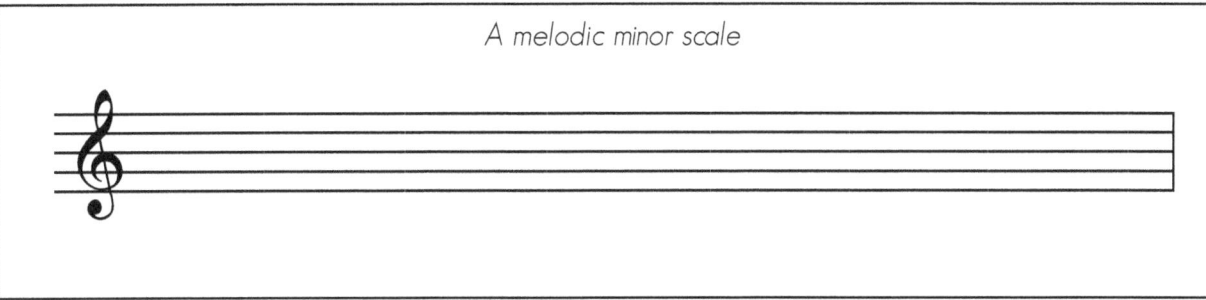

A melodic minor scale

E melodic minor scale

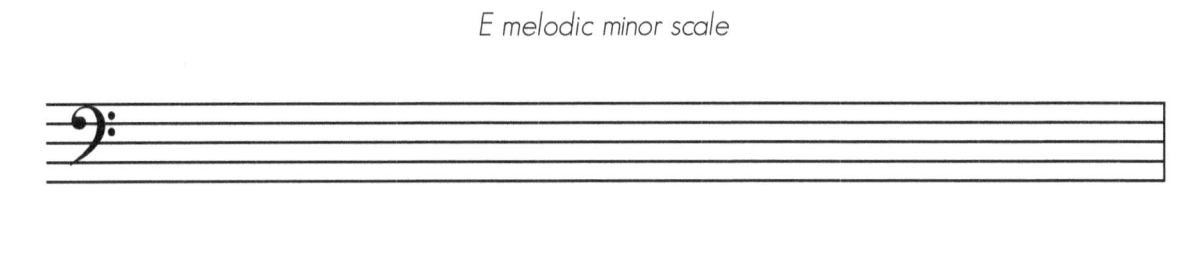

D melodic minor scale

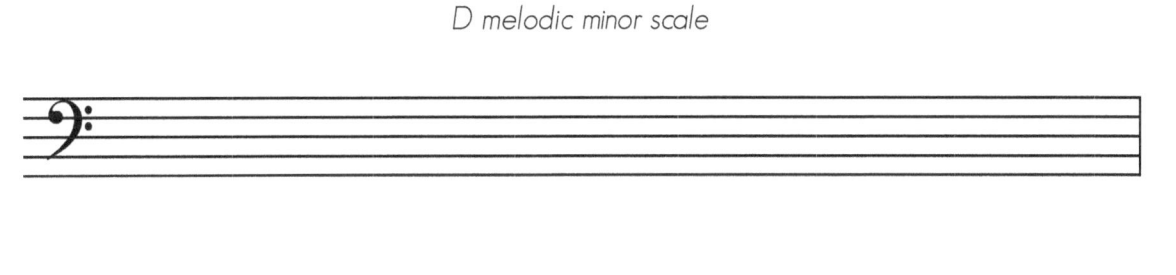

E harmonic minor scale

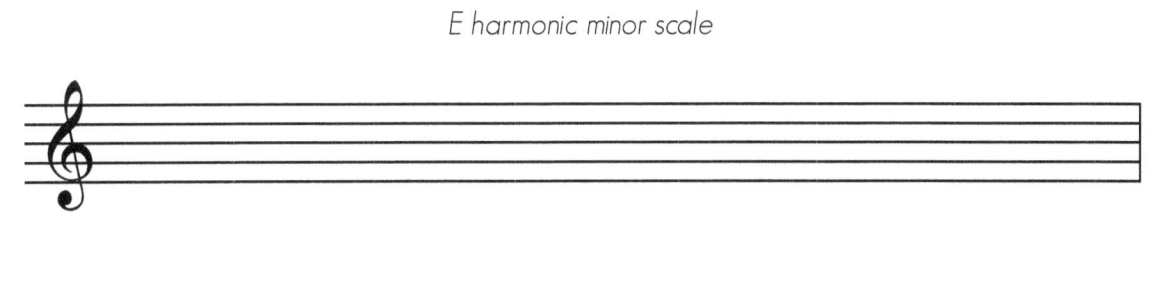

D harmonic minor scale

- Minor triads can be formed in the same way as major triads.
- A *tonic triad* is made up of three notes: the first, third and fifth note of the scale played in unison.
- In minor keys, these are the notes *la*, *do* and *mi*. You may know this combination of notes from playing arpeggios.

 Draw the triads below in the treble and bass clefs. Use key signatures.

A minor triad

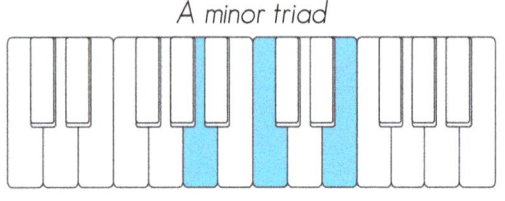  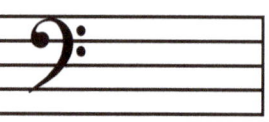

E minor triad

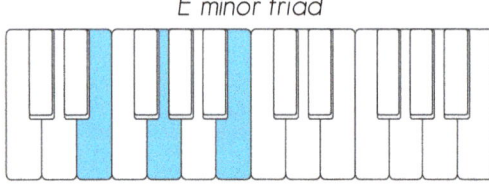  

D minor triad

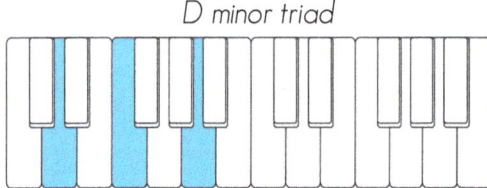  

- We can also form major and minor triads by remembering how many half steps there should be between each note.
- Major triads use intervals of 4 half steps, then 3 half steps.

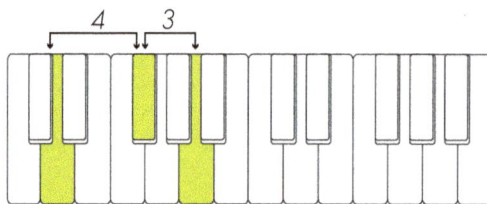

- Minor triads use intervals of 3 half steps, then 4 half steps.

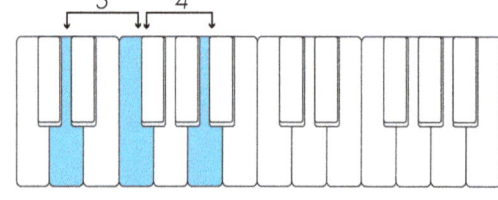

Thinking Theory Book Three — Chapter 5

 Count the half steps & circle either minor or major below each of these triads.

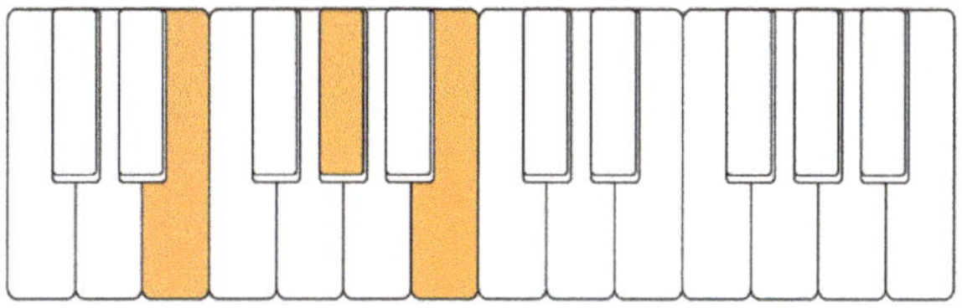

Major or Minor

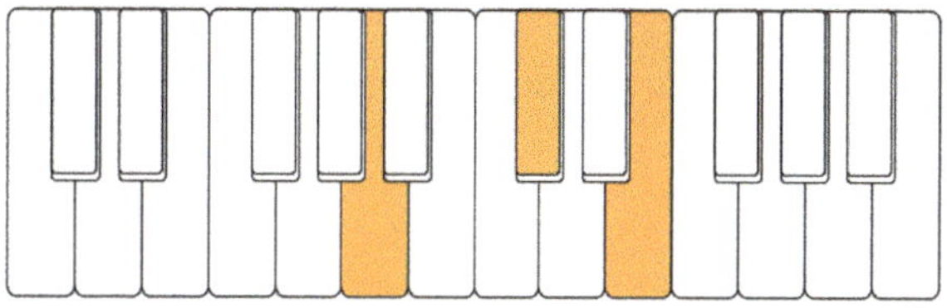

Major or Minor

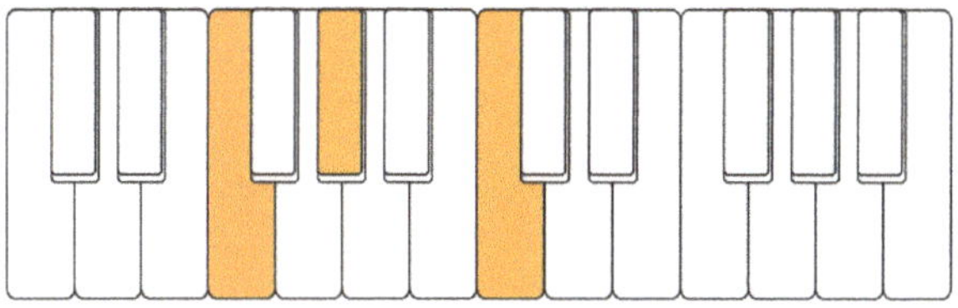

Major or Minor

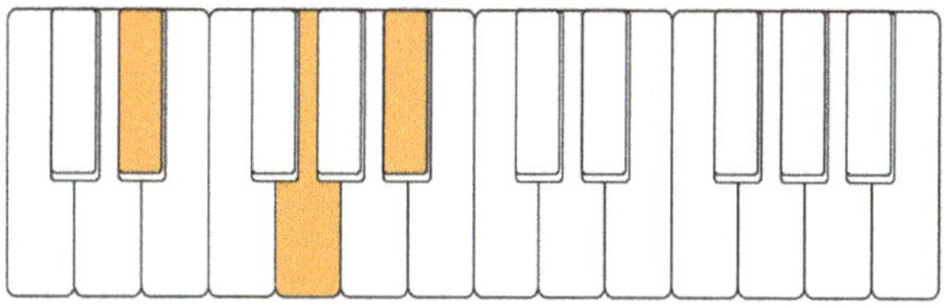

Major or Minor

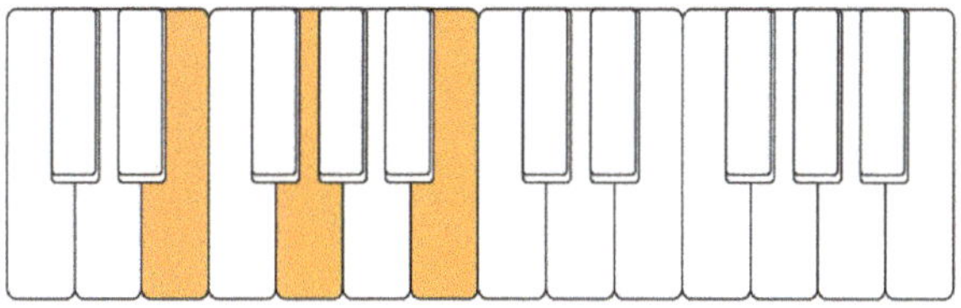

Major or Minor

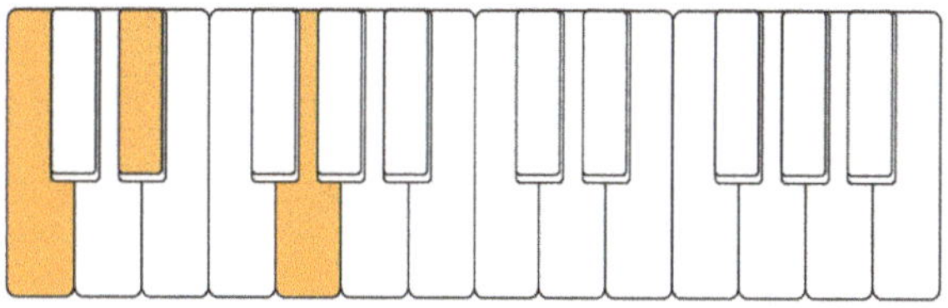

Major or Minor

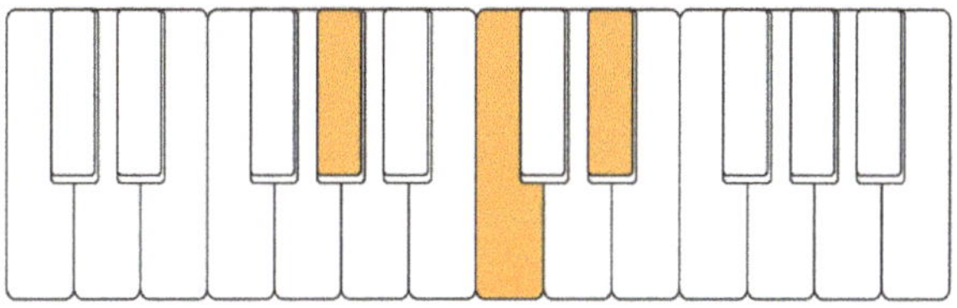

Major or Minor

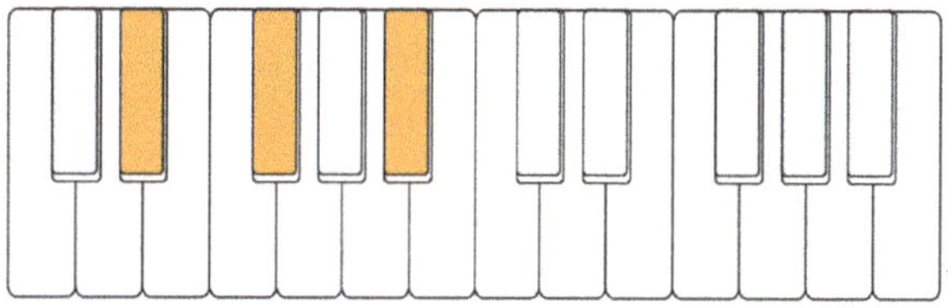

Major or Minor

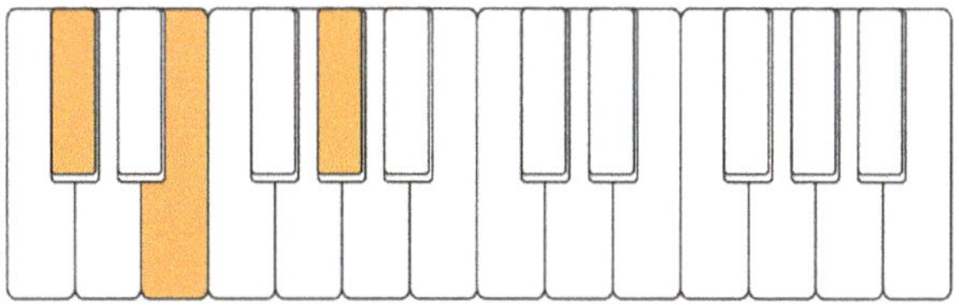

Major or Minor

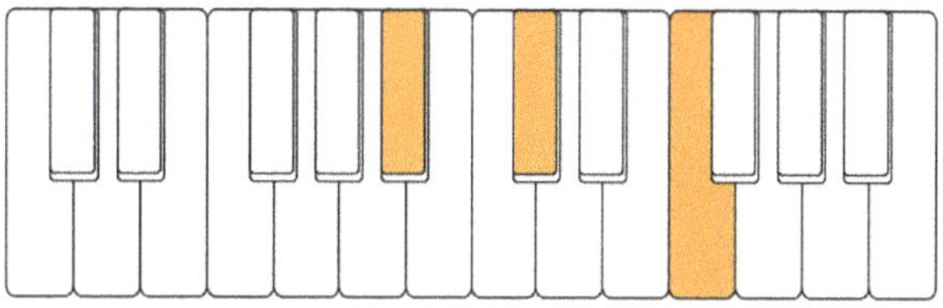

Major or Minor

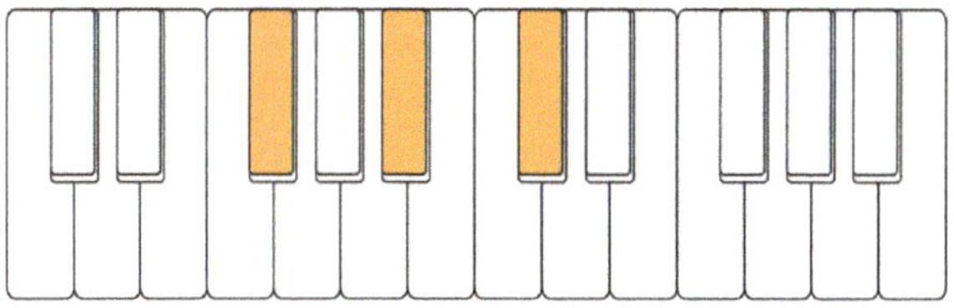

Major or Minor

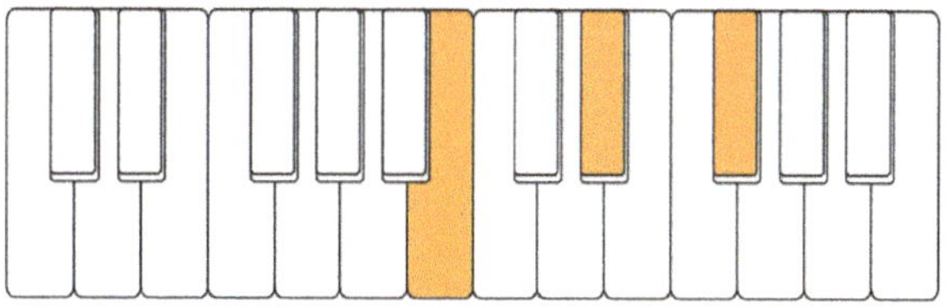

Major or Minor

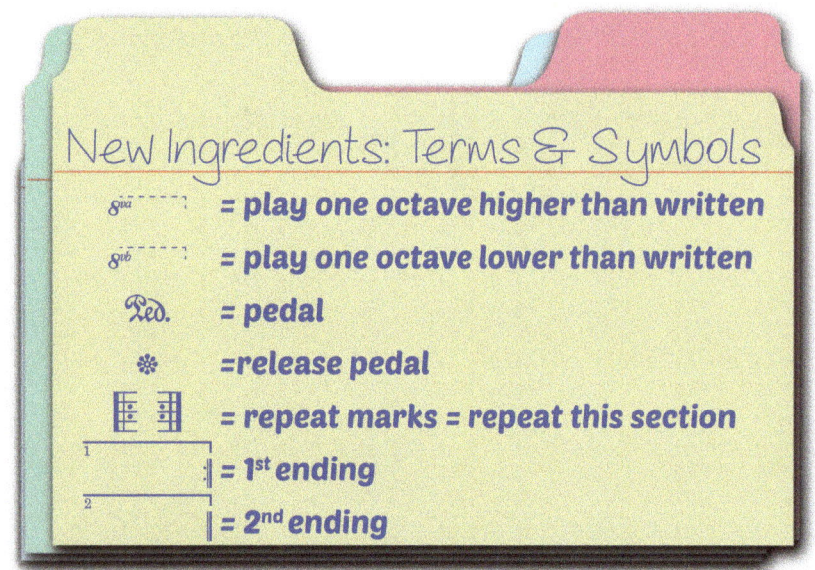

✏️ Add the missing barlines to the musical example below.

✏️ Add markings to the score below to show that:

1. Measures 1-4 should be played twice before measures 5-8 are played.
2. The pedal should be put down for measures 7-8.
3. The piece should be played slowly and sweetly.
4. The player should play softly from measures 1-4, gradually getting louder in measures 5-6, and ending the piece with measures 7-8 played moderately loudly.

✏️ Answer these questions about the piece.

1. What is the note name of the highest note in the piece? _____

2. Is the time signature duple, triple or quadruple? _____

3. What major key is the piece in? _____

Chapter 5

- Singing a melody using solfa will help you to compose an ending for it.
- Most melodies will sound best if they end on a long *do*.
- Draft your ideas in solfa stick notation before writing them on the staff.

✏️ Finish each melody by composing another two measures. Add a *tempo* mark above the staff, and a *dynamic* mark below the staff, to suit each melody.

Level Up!

Get ready for chapter 6 by answering these questions (without looking back through your book!)

1. Write each of these scales on the staff, ascending and descending. Use key signatures and mark the half steps.

A melodic minor

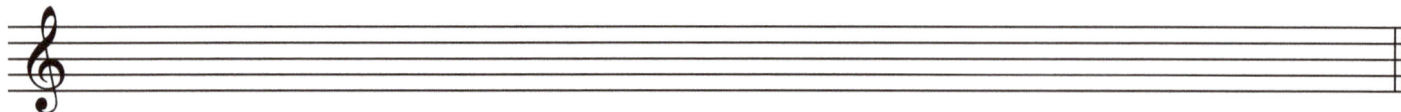

E harmonic minor

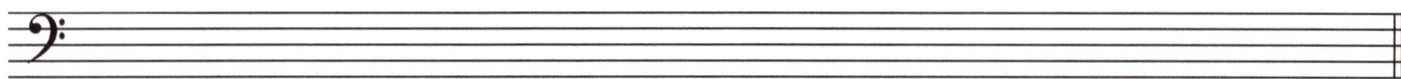

D melodic minor

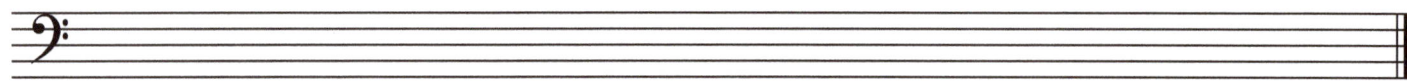

2. Draw the tonic triad in each of the major keys below.

3. Draw the tonic triad in each of the minor keys below.

4. What do these symbols mean?

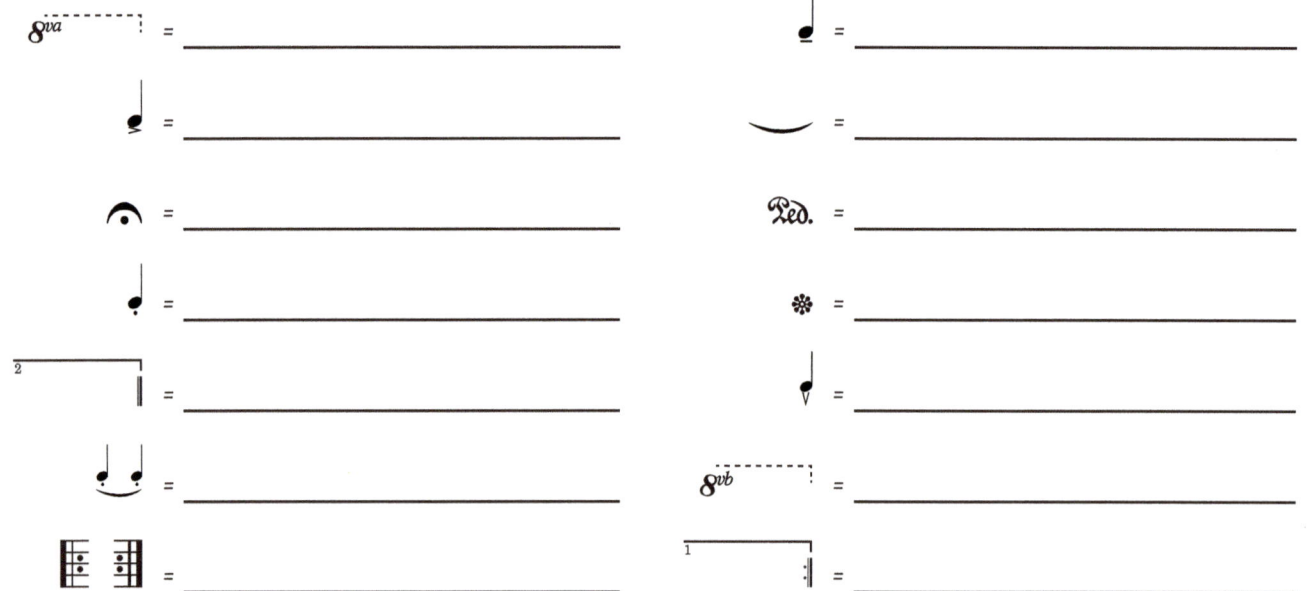

Level Up!
The final test! Answer these questions without looking back through your book!

1. Add a note above each of these notes to make harmonic intervals.

2. Draw the major triad to match each of these key signatures.

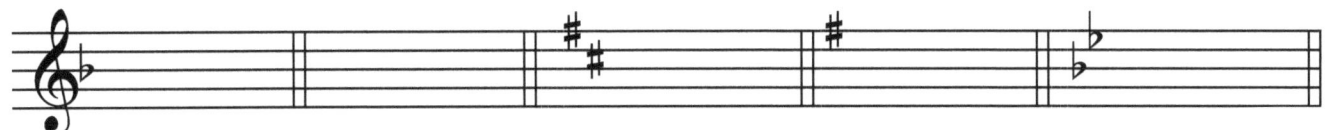

3. Draw the minor triad to match each of these key signatures.

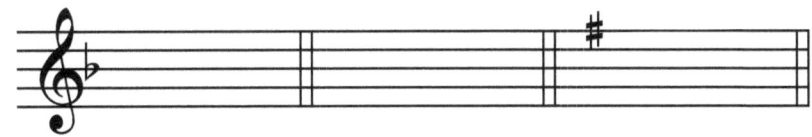

4. Write these notes with correct grouping on the staff below.
5.

6. Rewrite the melody at the same pitch in the bass clef.

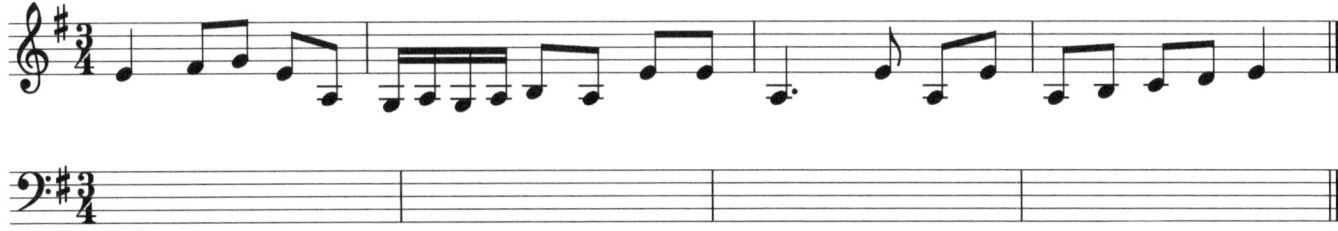

7. Add a rest or rests as needed at each arrow to complete the measures.

8. Write one octave of each of these scales. Use key signatures and mark the half steps.

E melodic minor ascending

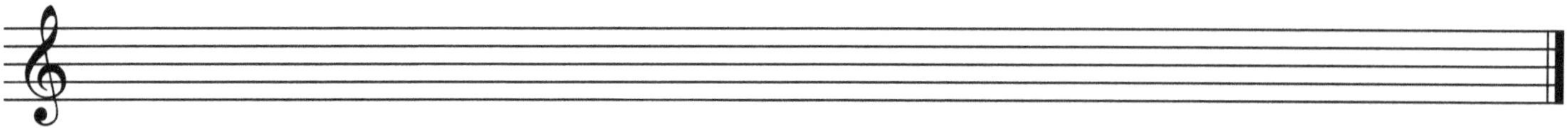

B♭ major ascending

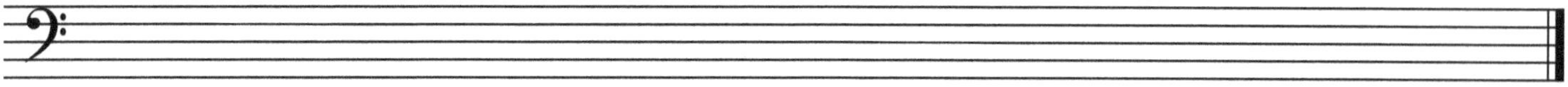

D harmonic minor descending

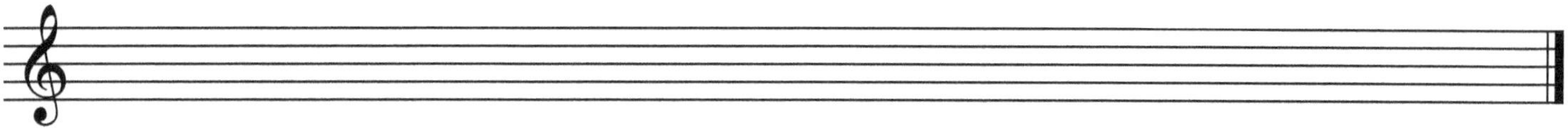

D major descending

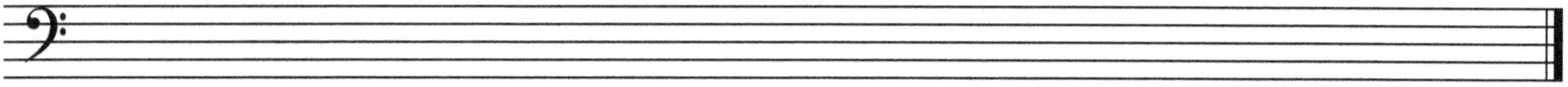

9. Name the keys of these melodies.

KEY:_____

KEY:_____

KEY:_____

KEY:_____

KEY:_____

10. Compose another two measures to finish this melody.

11. Add the missing time signature to this piece. Describe the time signature as duple, triple or quadruple.

_____

12. Add the missing barlines to this tune.

Answer questions 12, 13, and 14 about this piece.

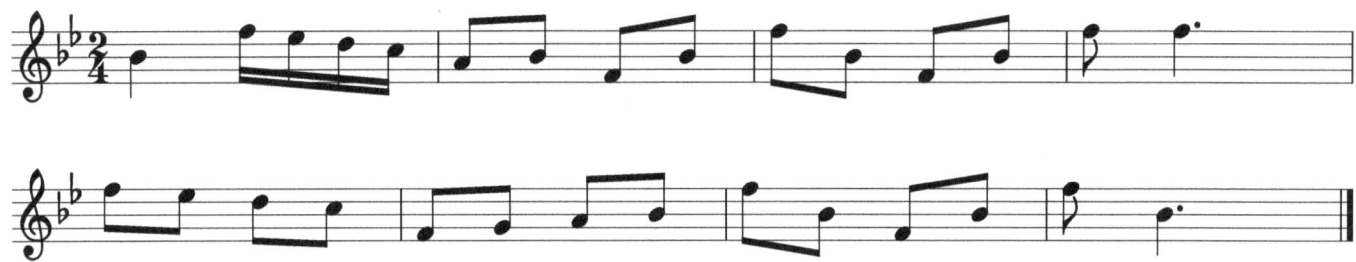

13. Add these to the piece:
    i.   Write a word above measure 1 to show that the music is to be played at a fast tempo.
    ii. Show that the music should begin moderately loudly.
    iii. Show that the music gets suddenly softer at measure 5.
    iv. Show that the last note is to be played very loudly.
    v.   Show that the performer should pause on the 'f' in measure 8.
    vi. Circle two consecutive notes which are a perfect fifth apart. Write "5" over the circle
    vii. Circle two consecutive notes which are a half step apart. Write "H" over the circle.

13. Complete these sentences:
    i.   The piece is in the key of ____ major.
    ii. The relative of this key is ____ minor.
    iii. Measure ____ has only notes from the tonic triad.

14. This is the beginning of the piece written in a different time signature. Complete the time signature. Continue the piece by writing measures 3 & 4 in the new time signature.

Term Review Cheat Sheet

♫	sixteenth note	¼ beat	*decresc.*	decrescendo	getting softer
♪	eighth note	½ beat	*rall.*	rallentando	getting slower
♪.	dotted eighth note	¾ beat	*rit.*	ritardando	getting slower
♫³	eighth note triplet	⅓ beat each	*ritard.*	ritardando	getting slower
♩	quarter note	1 beat	*poco rall.*	poco rallentando	getting a little slower
♩.	dotted quarter note	1 ½ beats	*poco rit.*	poco ritardando	getting a little slower
♩	half note	2 beats	*accelerando*		gradually getting faster
♩.	dotted half note	3 beats	*a tempo*		back to original speed
o	whole note	4 beats	*con moto*		with movement
𝄾	sixteenth rest	¼ beat	*meno mosso*		less movement
𝄾	eighth rest	½ beat	*più mosso*		more movement
𝄽	quarter rest	1 beat	♩	staccato	sharply detached
—	half rest	2 beats	♩	accent	with emphasis
—	whole rest	whole measure	♩	tenuto	with a fuller tone
2/4	simple duple time	2 quarter note beats in a measure	♩	marcato	with strong emphasis
3/4	simple triple time	3 quarter note beats in a measure	♩♩♩	portato/semi-staccato	slightly detached
4/4	simple quadruple time	4 quarter note beats in a measure	⌢	fermata	pause
C	common time	4 quarter note beats in a measure	⌢	slur	play smoothly
¢	cut time	2 half note beats in a measure	𝄆 𝄇	repeat marks	repeat this section
2/2	simple duple time	2 half note beats in a measure	8va		one octave higher than written
3/2	simple triple time	3 half note beats in a measure	8vb		one octave lower than written
4/2	simple quadruple time	4 half note beats in a measure	1.		1st ending
3/8	simple triple time	3 eighth note beats in a measure	2.		2nd ending
enharmonic		same sound written differently	℘ed.		depress sustain pedal
half step		notes directly beside each other	❋		release sustain pedal
whole step		two half steps	*presto*		fast
♯	sharp	one half step higher	*vivace*		lively
♭	flat	one half step lower	*allegro*		quick & lively
♮	natural	not sharp or flat	*allegretto*		moderately quick
pp	pianissimo	very soft	*moderato*		moderate speed
p	piano	soft	*alla marcia*		like a march
sempre p	sempre piano	always soft	*andante*		walking pace
mp	mezzo piano	moderately soft	*larghetto*		fairly slowly
mf	mezzo forte	moderately loud	*largo*		slowly
f	forte	loud	*adagio*		slowly
sempre f	sempre forte	always loud	*lento*		slowly
ff	fortissimo	very loud	*dolce*		sweetly
sf	sforzando	emphasized	*grazioso*		gracefully
fp	fortepiano	loud then immediately soft	*cantabile*		with a singing tone
<	crescendo	getting louder	*giocoso*		playful/merry
>	diminuendo	getting softer	*maestoso*		majestic
cresc.	crescendo	getting louder	*espressivo*		expressive
dim.	diminuendo	getting softer			

Certificate of Achievement

Congratulations to

_____
(Student Name)

for successfully completing Thinking Theory Book Three

Date completed: _____

Teacher's signature: _____

What is Thinking Theory?

➡ Thinking Theory is a series of music theory workbooks, designed to accelerate learning while providing plenty of reinforcement of each concept.

➡ All concepts are presented in a clear and concise way and page layouts are clean and consistent.

➡ No topic is introduced without being revisited several times later in the book.

➡ Thinking Theory is designed so you can start anywhere in the series. Concepts are not left out of later books, just covered more quickly.

➡ The flashcard games provide a unique way to learn away from the page, and make learning and teaching more secure and more fun.

➡ The "Level Up!" tests at the end of each chapter and book allow you to evaluate student learning and plan their next step.

➡ The Thinking Theory Plus books provide a lateral move for students who have finished one book but are not quite ready for the next.

➡ Singing with solfa (movable do) is integrated into the theory books. Solfa helps students with ear training, transposing, sight reading and composition.

Core Thinking Theory Books

Thinking Theory Plus Books

www.colourfulkeys.ie